Beckoning Aspirations
Solving the Assyrian Resource Dilemma

Naramsen Goriel

Beckoning Aspirations
Solving the Assyrian Resource Dilemma

ISBN: 978-0-9963012-3-7

TABLE OF CONTENTS

PREFACE

In June of 2014, after a startling military offensive by the Islamic State, ISIL gained controlled of Mosul, an Iraqi city within the Nineveh Province. From 2014 to 2018, ISIL has destroyed Assyrian archaeological sites in Mosul; around the same time, Iraq's federal government and Islamic State forces have fought for control of Tikrit and Anbar Province.[1] Coalition and Iraq government forces battled for eight months and immobilized ISIL near the Tigris river, claiming victory for the city of Mosul, but displacing many Assyrians while accumulating billions of dollars in infrastructure damage.[2] Ensuring further uncertainty for Assyrians was an illegal Kurdish backed independence referendum staged by Kurdish Regional Government which forced the Iraqi federal government to intervene with an offensive driving back Kurdish annexation. Despite preventing the referendum, discrimination against Assyrian people continues.

With Assyrians placed in different circumstances in different countries as a result of being caught within a spiral of war, oppression, and genocide, Assyrians around the world yearn for an independent Assyrian state. Assyrian political organizations have helped draw attention to the Assyrian cause, and educated, diligent, and patient groups of Assyrians must arise, capable of assisting their fellow Assyrians around the world. In order for Assyrians to succeed, those educated, wealthy, and sophisticated Assyrians who live in a post-industrial world must unite without boundaries, narcissism, tribal conflicts, religious division, and nationality toward individual millets. If these reasonable terms can be fulfilled, then Assyrians will be successful in embracing unity under any circumstance even if simultaneously being persecuted.

All things considered, Assyrians will experience challenging junctures no matter their surroundings until the community, undivided,

---

[1] https://www.bbc.com/news/world-middle-east-14546763
[2] https://www.reuters.com/article/us-mideast-crisis-iraq-aid/basic-infrastructure-repair-in-mosul-will-cost- over-1-billion-u-n-idUSKBN19Q28F

progresses in learning to organize enthusiastic intellectual Assyrian inclusively to accumulate and sustain resources, and identify common grievances with conviction.

In 2003, an enthusiastic Assyrian population missed the opportunity and to benefit from the ousting of Saddam Hussein's dictatorship and establish legitimate authority in the Nineveh Province. Despite this opportunity, Assyrian political organizations did not take advantage of this possibility, consequently causing a disparity between Assyrian aspirations and real Assyrian sensibility. Often, when expectations are substantially different from current realities, it is an indication that something is profoundly wrong and reform is needed.

This book is not about blame but rather concerns the circumstances that have placed the Assyrians in dire circumstances, particularly the external and internal factors, precluding Assyrian progress. Such factors ask what are the consequences of the millet system? What is the Assyrian resource dilemma? How can Assyrian learn to accumulate resources together in a diaspora? How has terrorism affected Assyrians in an already chaotic region? How will Assyrians alleviate the effect of globalization? Are Assyrians being vindictive? Are they allowing feelings of spite and ambition to get in the way of rational thinking? How much is an Assyrian willing to sacrifice to achieve the goal of Assyrian development?

I will argue that Assyrian developments are profoundly skewed toward spite and ambition, which inevitably will deepen discontent. The future is uncertain, of course, but despite the totality of circumstances, indications are that a revival of Assyrian development is possible. There is an opportunity for Assyrians to redefine who they are, why they have joined together, and what they owe each other. Assyrians can, if they choose, "assert that their mutual obligations as citizens extend beyond economic usefulness to one another, and act accordingly."[3] Despite obstacles, Assyrians living in a diaspora have the ability to cooperate and integrate politically toward learning how to allocate resources for the well-being of all Assyrians, specifically those who are vulnerable and overlooked. The quantity of resources is important but can be ancillary if an efficient scheme is created to administer resources adequately. However, without sufficient democratic principles, reasonable nationalism, and political reform of regional political integration and international cooperation, an Assyrian breakthrough will not be possible.

---

[3] Robert Reich. The Work of Nations. Pg. 310. New York: First Vintage edition, 1992.

INTRODUCTION

The Middle East stands out as one of the more ethnically and religiously heterogeneous regions in the world. The overwhelming majority of the citizens of the region are religiously Muslim and ethnically Arab, Persian, or Turkish. The Assyrian indigenous minority is unique because it is not categorized under these ethnic and religious classifications. Within this area, Assyrians are among the smallest and least visible groups.

The Assyrians are an indigenous, Semitic-speaking (Aramaic) people who are predominantly Christian, and their history in the Middle East spans more than 5000 years. The term "Assyrian" also refers to Chaldean (Roman Catholic) and Syriac (Orthodox), which are religious identifications commonly used by those religious sects. In evaluations and research on the various ethnicities that comprise the Middle East, the Assyrian people have been largely overlooked because of their modest size—the Assyrian population ranges from one to three million around the world. Although it is, for the most part, disregarded in the present day, Assyrian history has demonstrated that the Assyrians helped to cultivate and sophisticate legal philosophies throughout the years, which are still in use today. All things considered, the Assyrian people have survived the defeat of the ancient Assyrian Empire and acts of oppression and genocide at the hands of ruling empires and invaders. Despite the divisive, hostile policies of the Ottoman Empire and dictatorships, Assyrians have kept their culture and Neo-Assyrian dialect intact, abstaining from the influences of the rise of Islam and the subsequent Arabization and Kurdification of the region.

International law supports order in the world and the attainment of humanity's fundamental goals of peace, prosperity, respect for human rights, and protection of the natural environment. Unfortunately, Assyrian progress has been precluded by oppression, genocide, discrimination, and lack of representation. Furthermore, the international community has largely ignored the rights of the Assyrian people. This work discusses the circumstances that the Assyrian people have endured and poses the following question: Why does the international community ignore the legal and human rights of a group of people that have presented great benefit to civilization through their significant intellectual contributions? Furthermore, this paper discusses the struggle for Assyrian political organizations to maintain adequate resources to culminate progress toward an Assyrian state. The sources of this book relate to more than a decade of research, from September 2004 to March 2018. However, these sources remain imperfect and incomplete. All of my conclusions are tenuous and are open to be questioned and debated.

Furthermore, it is important to note that social science is not an actual science. Social science cannot accurately predict human behavior through a mathematical formula.[4] Therefore, it is essential to understand the complexities of authority, legitimacy, governments, economics and not intertwine actual science discipline with social science studies. Social science is designed to test one's assumptions regarding actual truth, knowledge, and beliefs. Research in the field of social science does not adopt the purpose of "producing mathematical certainties that can replace democratic debate in which all opinions are represented."[5]

The first part of this work will focus on the history of Assyrian authority figures reforming Assyrian institutions, and its impact on the Middle East, the history of the Assyrian Church of the East, the modern history of Assyrians, a brief summary and timeline of the US-led invasion on Iraq, the creation and operations of the Islamic State of Iraq and the Levant, and the facts provided from data that provide evidence of undue persecution of the Assyrian people in the Middle East.

The latter portion of this work defines the Assyrian resource dilemma and proposes an Assyrian national bargain and a recommendation of how Assyrians can learn to unify resources to help their cause for autonomy and prosperity.

---

[4] Thomas Piketty. Capital in the Twenty-First Century. P. 571
[5] Ibid.

SECTION I—ASSYRIAN HISTORY

CHAPTER ONE – ANCIENT ASSYRIAN HISTORY

The Assyrians originated between the Tigris and the Euphrates rivers in what is now modern-day Iraq, and they are among the indigenous peoples in present-day Iraq, northwestern Iran, northeastern Syria, and southeastern Turkey. Contemporary Assyrians are direct descendants of the Ancient Assyrian people from the upper Tigris River in Iraq. Through geological and archeological discoveries, the existence of the ancient Assyrian civilization has been proven through the findings of old documentation, ancient artifacts, sculptures, palaces, and portions of ancient cities. [6]

The Assyrian Empire was the first documented civilization. It was located in Assyria (Mesopotamia), which is widely known as the cradle of civilization. Different segments of Assyrians (Assyrians, Sumerians, Akkadians, and Babylonians) ruled the empire, and Assyrians as a whole excelled in the development of advanced agriculture and mathematics and the creation of a system of governance, a code of laws, the first library, scientific medicine, architecture, a practical system of writing such as pictographs and cuneiform, and the most advanced military of its time.[7]

Code of Hammurabi (1700 BC – 1300 BC) – Legal Reform
The Code of Hammurabi is an example that demonstrates the development of laws that set societal boundaries in densely populated cities such as Babylon. Hammurabi's counterpart, Shamshi-Adad I, implemented a similar code of laws in the northern city of Nineveh around the same period that the Code of Hammurabi was implemented. [8]

---

[6] Joel Elias. "The Genetics of Modern Assyrians and Their Relationship to Other People of the Middle East." University of California School of Medicine, San Francisco. July 2000

[7] Sargon Dadesho. The Assyrian National Question. Bet-Nahrain Press. 1988

[8] C. H. W. Johns. Babylonian and Assyrian Laws, Contracts and Letters (1904). Shamshi-Adad I (fl. late 18th century BC) was an ancient king from the Near East. After his death, the empire was soon defeated by Hammurabi of Babylon and came under the control of the First Babylonian Dynasty throughout this period. He was incorporated into the traditional lists of kings of Assyria, and earlier archaeologists assumed he was indeed Assyrian.

The Code was inscribed in stone. The set of laws encouraged citizens of Babylon to accept the authority of the king, who was trying to establish common rules to govern subjects' behavior. [9] The Code of Hammurabi begins with a prologue, which describes the time in which Hammurabi first became king, as evident in this quote:

> Anu (King of Anunaki) and Bel (Lord of Heaven and Earth) called by name me, Hammurabi, the exalted prince ... to bring about the rule of righteousness in the land to destroy the wicked and the evildoers so that the strong should not harm the weak, so that I should rule over the black-headed people like Shamash and enlighten the land to further the well-being of mankind.

The actual rules range from public to private matters, with humane approaches to human problems. The laws deal with marriage and family relations; negligence; fraud; commercial contracts; duties of public officials; property and inheritance; crimes and punishments; techniques of legal procedure; protection for women, children, and slaves; fairness in commercial exchange; protection of property; standard procedures for adjudicating disputes; and debt relief for victims of food and drought. Additionally, the list explains in detail each and every one of the instances in which the laws would apply. [10]

The penalties of the code varied according to the status of the victim. Babylonian society included three classes: the patricians, who were free men and women; the plebeians, who were commoners; and the slaves.[11] While the law of retaliation protected the patricians, the lower classes received only monetary compensation.

The purpose of the Code of Hammurabi was to exercise political power to create common bonds among the diverse people

---

[9] Jean Boterro. The Near East: The Early Civilizations (1967).
[10] Ibid.
[11] "Hammurabi and the End of His Dynasty," Cambridge Ancient History, rev. ed., Vol. 2, Ch. 5 (1965).

who comprised this ancient society.[12]   The historic code of laws cultivated by Hammurabi and his advisors helped unify the empire by offering standards for moral values, class structure, relationships between genders, and religion. The Code of Hammurabi was one of the most important Mesopotamian contributions to civilization because it provided public services, settled conflicts, and set up a common defense coupled with a platform of precepts to assist predecessors to reform the Assyrian empire when necessary.

Post-Hammurabi (1690 BC – 610 BC) – Reforming the Military

The Assyrian Empire ruled the Near East for thousands of years following the issuance of the Code of Hammurabi. Throughout the different eras, the Assyrian Empire revised, redacted, and re-created different laws that affected society. For example, Tiglath-Pileser III, who ruled from 745–727 BC, implemented two major reforms to the Assyrian Empire. One of the first reforms related to governors' powers within the provinces of Assyria. Tiglath-Pileser III reduced the size of the provinces and appointed his own governors, who were required to report to the king concerning the collection and the amounts of taxation, storage of military resources, and security for merchants. The governors effectively limited the power of the provinces through the decrease in the size of the overall population, which precluded the effective production of resources. Tiglath-Pileser III commandeered the Assyrian provinces and their resources through delegation of authority from his appointed governors. This reform of provincial boundaries and resource control established hegemony for the king[13] by limiting opposition to the point of congregation and revolt.

The second reform concerned the defense and security of the kingdom. Tiglath-Pileser III replaced a seasonal conscripted army with a standing professional army. The new "Assyrian army transitioned to a skilled professional force when compared with its predecessor, which had relied on somewhat haphazard conscription."[14] The new military policy included a new "intelligence system using reports transmitted by

---

[12] Pedersén Olof (1998). Archives and Libraries in the Ancient Near East:1500-300 B.C.
[13] Henry Saggs. The Might That Was Assyria (London, 1984).
[14] Ibid.

12

staging posts."[15]

The king incorporated large numbers of conquered people into the army, thus adding a substantial foreign element. This force primarily comprised the infantry, whereas the native Assyrians comprised the cavalry and engineers of sophisticated chariots. As a result of Tiglath- Pileser's military reforms, the Assyrian Empire was armed with a greatly expanded army that was capable of campaigning throughout the year. The addition of the cavalry and the chariot contingents to the army was largely due to the steppe cultures lurking nearby to the north, who occasionally invaded the northern lands, relying primarily upon cavalry and primitive chariots.[16] All in all, Tiglath-Pileser III's reforms were a transcendence and progression from the Code of Hammurabi to conform the Assyrian empire to the natural changes of society.

End of the Assyrian Empire (606 BC) – Reform and millet system

The Assyrians' sophisticated society, coupled with dominant and diligent monarchs, helped them to become the strongest empire in the Near East for centuries. The Assyrian conquests spread civilization to formerly unfamiliar lands. This aspect of the Assyrian Empire is often overshadowed by scholars' preoccupation with the Assyrian military machine and its so- called "barbaric behavior." Indeed, the Assyrians never conquered and destroyed; "they conquered and civilized, teaching their subjects the art of the highest civilization then in existence."[17] The cultural unification of the Middle East is a subtle concept to grasp, yet it must be understood that it was the greatest achievement of the Assyrians. In 606 B.C., the Assyrian Empire fell because of internal leadership problems, in conjunction with opposing empires that applied financial and military pressure to the Assyrian empire, thereby causing its collapse.

---

15 Ibid.
16 Tadmor Hayim, The Inscriptions of Tiglath-Pileser III, King of Assyria: Critical Edition, with Introductions, Translations, and Commentary (Jerusalem, Israel Academy of Sciences and Humanities, 1994)
17 Henry Saggs, Everyday Life in Babylonia and Assyria. Assyrian National News Agency. 196

The fall of the Assyrian Empire did not mean the end of the Assyrian people, however. The Assyrian people were predominantly peasant farmers, and, because Assyria contains some of the best wheat land in the Near East, descendants of the Assyrian peasants built new villages over old cities as opportunity permitted and carried on with their agricultural life, incorporating traditions from the former cities. After seven or eight centuries and various vicissitudes, these people became Christians, and the Christian and Jewish communities scattered amongst them, not only keeping alive the memory of their Assyrian predecessors but also combining them with traditions that were guided by spiritual beliefs. In turn, the spiritual beliefs induced a cultural transition from a secular dominant Assyrian society to a faith-based religious society.

CHAPTER TWO - ASSYRIAN CHURCH HISTORY

During the early years of the Common Era in 33 A.D., the Assyrian nation accepted Christianity, after King Abgar Okama accepted Christ and his origins based upon correspondence between Christ and King Abgar.[18] After their acceptance of Christianity, the Assyrians established the Assyrian Apostolic Church of the East, which was founded through its apostolic origins by St. Peter, St. Thomas, and St. Thaddeus. The first congregation existed around 100 A.D. in Edessa, and the Assyrian Church of the East was later established in Selucia-Ctesphon. The church maintained its presence in Selucia-Ctesphon until 779 A.D. The Church of the East had 80 million members and 19 archbishops, and, collectively, they spread Christianity east toward Mongolia, China, and India.[19]

As Christianity spread and empires proceeded in accepting the faith, many different interpretations began to percolate. Around 300 A.D., Constantine, the Emperor of Rome, freely allowed Christianity to replace Roman polytheism with the monotheistic faith. Despite the strong Christian faith, various interpretations of the study of Christ gained strength. In other words, there was intense study of Christ's human nature, his divine nature, and the interrelationship between these two natures as well as how they interacted and affected each other. This polarization of Christianity throughout the centuries caused the Assyrian Church of the East to lose members. However, the Church of the East established authority and maintained its authority with the Assyrian people.

Episcopal polity governs the Church of the East, as is the case with other Catholic churches.[20] The church maintains a system of geographical parishes organized into dioceses and archdioceses. The Catholicos-Patriarch is head of the church. The synod is comprised of bishops who oversee individual dioceses & metropolitans who oversee

---

[18] Samuel Moffet, A History of Christianity in Asia: Beginnings to 1500. Harper Collins Press.1992
[19] Mark Dickens, "The Church of the East." The American Foundation for Syriac Studies. October 2012
[20] Catholic refers to the term "universal."

Episcopal dioceses under their territorial jurisdiction.[21]

At the turn of the century, the patriarchate of the Church of the East was located in Qudshanis in the Hakkari Mountains. The language of the Assyrian Church of the East is classical Aramaic, its worship is sacramental and liturgical, its theology is in accordance with the Nicene Creed and the teaching of the fathers of the Church, its customs are Semitic, and its present attitude toward other Christians is ecumenical. It exists primarily in Iraq, Iran, Syria, and Lebanon but also in Europe, North America, Australia, and India.

The church and the Assyrian community in general faced considerable fragmentation and upheaval as a result of the conflicts of the twentieth century; the Assyrian patriarch at the time, Mar Shimun, was forced to reorganize the church's structure in the United States. He transferred his residence to San Francisco, California, in 1954, and traveled to Iran, Lebanon, Kuwait, and India, where he worked to strengthen the church. In 1964, he decreed a number of changes to the church, including liturgical reform, the adoption of the Gregorian calendar, and the shortening of Lent. These changes, combined with Shimun's long absence from Iraq, caused a rift in the community, which led to another schism. In 1968, traditionalists within the church elected Mar Thoma Darmo as a rival patriarch to Shimun, thus creating the Ancient Church of the East.

In 1972, Shimun decided to step down as patriarch, and, the following year, he married in contravention to longstanding church custom. This led to a synod in 1973, following which further reforms were introduced, the most significant of which was the permanent abolition of hereditary succession, a practice introduced in the middle of the fifteenth century by the patriarch Shemon IV Basidi who died in 1497. It was eventually decided that Shimun should be reinstated, and this matter was to have been settled at additional synods in 1975. However, an estranged relative assassinated Shimun before this could take place.

---

[21] Mar Aprem Mooken, The Assyrian Church of the East in the Twentieth Century. St. Ephrem Ecumenical Research Institute, 2003.

In 1976, the patriarch of the Assyrian Church of the East, Mar Dinkha IV, was elected as Shimun's successor. The 33-year-old Dinkha had previously been metropolitan of Tehran, and he operated his See there until the Iran-Iraq War of 1980–1988. Thereafter, Mar Dinkha IV went into exile in the United States and transferred the patriarchal See to Chicago. Much of his patriarchate has been concerned with tending to the Assyrian Diaspora community in the wake of Saddam Hussein's attacks on the Kurds during and after the Iran-Iraq War and with strengthening ecumenical relations with other churches.

In 2015, Mar Dinkha IV passed away of natural causes. On September 2015, the church appointed successor as the patriarch of the Assyrian Church of the East, Mar Gewargis Sliwa, and relocated its structure back to its origins in the Middle East.[22]

---

[22] Masoud Barzani. Twitter Post. September 28 2015, 6:25 a.m. http://twitter.com/masoud_barzani/

CHAPTER THREE - MODERN ASSYRIAN HISTORY

The Millet System

Following the rise of Islam, the Assyrians lived in confessional communities, which are comprised of groups of people living together and sharing their religious beliefs.[23] This type of organizational structure is referred to as a millet system. This structure was primarily dominant during the reign of the Ottoman Empire, when communities were autonomous from Ottoman law and were able to govern themselves under their own system.[24]

The Assyrians were bound to their respective millets by their religious affiliations rather than their ethnic origins, according to the millet concept. The Assyrians would elect Maliks, which means "kings" in Aramaic, to become the principal leaders of the millets. The head of the millet would communicate directly to the Ottoman sultan and the Sassanid king, respectively.[25]

The millet system divided the Assyrians into different regions of the Middle East. Within those regions, the Assyrian millets established their own pluralistic society, and each millet shared resources reciprocally with the other millets. The millets' socioeconomic status was meager, and the location of the millets was remote, although near enemy tribes. Most roads were impassable, and the winters in the northern Hakkari Mountains were brutal. Nevertheless, the Assyrian millets maintained their autonomy, their culture, and their livelihood. During the reign of the Ottoman Empire up until the end of World War II, millets controlled the conscription and mobilization of an Assyrian army, as well as overall commerce, and provided protection and services to the other Assyrian millets, many of whom were less fortunate.

---

[23] Sachedina Abdulaziz Abdulhussein (2001). The Islamic Roots of Democratic Pluralism. Oxford University Press.
[24] Benjamin Braude and Bernard Lewis (ed.), Christians and Jews in the Ottoman Empire. The Functioning of a Plural Society, 2 vol., New York and London, 1982.
[25] Ibid.

There were advantages and disadvantages to the millet system for Assyrians. One advantage of the millet system was the autonomy to govern and structure society based upon Christian principles and beliefs rather than Islamic principles. The millet system permitted minority jurisdiction pertaining to personal legal concepts familiar to Assyrians, rather than the Ottoman rule of law. Another advantage of the millet system was that the structure allowed for the Assyrians to maintain their origins and beliefs, despite the fact that different ethnicities and religious groups surrounded the millet borders. The final advantage to the millet system was that it allowed the Assyrians to collect their own taxes. In other words, the Assyrian millet structure was democratic in its practices within an absolute monarchy.

The disadvantages of the millet system were numerous. The most evident disadvantage of the millet system was that the structure of rule of law served as a mechanism to divide and conquer the minorities within the Ottoman Empire. Many Assyrians were hundreds and thousands of miles away from family, relatives, business partners, church congregations, and friends. The communal division hindered Assyrian society and collective progression. Furthermore, the negative effects of the divide-and-conquer practice were demonstrably apparent, as tribal conflicts between different Assyrians began to ensue. The conflicts were generally based on millets' divergences over land and disputes over farm animals and the amount of taxes to be collected.

Another disadvantage of the millet system was its legal inconsistency. Because there were many different millets and tribes within the Assyrian community, each was required to govern its own society. This resulted in a less uniform Assyrian community, which caused resources to be scarce. For example, some millets were in northern mountainous regions and conformed to their environment, setting security and safety as top priorities for their millet, while other millets near developed cities valued commerce and trade.

All millets had a great deal of power, setting their own laws and collecting and distributing their own taxes. When a member of one millet committed a crime against a member of some other millet, the law of the injured party applied. However, because the ruling Islamic majority was paramount, any dispute involving a Muslim fell under the empire's Sharia-based law.[26]

Reform is common with Assyrians because Assyrians have conformed their culture to the dynamic change in their livelihood throughout centuries. Thus, reform is a practice familiar to Assyrian institutions and their members. However, external factors beyond the control of Assyrian institutions have hindered development. Factors such as discrimination, genocide, world wars, foreign influence and geographic displacement have caused shock and stagnation to 21st century reformation. Additionally, the inconspicuous properties of oppression such as demagoguery, self-loathing and internalized oppression have induced multifarious resentment toward similar Assyrian groups.

---

[26] Ilber Ortayh (2006), Son İmparatorluk Osmanlı [The Last Empire: Ottoman Empire] İstanbul: Timaş Yayınları (Timaş Press), pp. 87–89

CHAPTER FOUR – THE ASSYRIAN GENOCIDE AND BRTISH MANDATE

The Assyrian population in the Ottoman Empire numbered about one million at the turn of the twentieth century and was largely concentrated in what is now Iran, Iraq, and Turkey. There were also hundreds of thousands of Maronite Christians in Lebanon who had some Assyrian heritage but who are less often called Assyrians. As with other Christians residing in the empire, they were treated as second-class citizens and were denied public positions of power. Violence directed against them prior to the First World War was not new. Many Assyrians were subjected to Kurdish brigandage and even outright massacre and forced conversion to Islam, as was the case with the Assyrians of Hakkari during the massacres of Badr Khan in the 1840s and the Massacres of Diyarbakır during the 1895–1896 Hamidian Massacres.[27] The Hamidiye received assurances from the Ottoman Sultan that they could kill Assyrians and Armenians with impunity, and they were particularly active in Urhoy and Diyarbakir.

The Ottoman Empire began massacring Assyrians in the nineteenth century, a time of friendly relations between the Ottomans and the British, who were defending the Ottomans from the Russian Empire's efforts to include under its protection the communities of Ottoman Orthodox Christians. In October 1914, the Ottoman Empire began deporting and massacring Assyrians and Armenians in Van.[28] After attacking Russian cities and declaring war on Britain and France, the empire declared a holy war on Christians. The German Kaiser and the German Ambassador to the Ottoman Empire directed and orchestrated the holy war and financed the Ottomans' war against the Russian Empire.[29]

---

[27] Hannibal Travis. Genocide in the Middle East: The Ottoman Empire, Iraq, and Sudan. Durham, NC: Carolina Academic Press, 2010.
[28] Ibid. pp. 237–77, 293–294.
[29] Anahit Khosoreva, "The Assyrian Genocide in the Ottoman Empire and Adjacent Territories," from The Armenian Genocide: Cultural and Ethical Legacies. Ed. Richard G. Hovannisian. New Brunswick, NJ: Transaction Publishers, 2007

The earliest programs of extermination took place in the southern province of Diyarbakir, under the direction of Reshid Bey. The commander of Ottoman Army Group East declared in his memoirs that his forces accounted for 300,000 deaths in Diyarbakir and elsewhere. Reports from a German consul and a vice-consul accounted in 1915 that Assyrians were being massacred in Diyarbakır, Harput, Mardin, and Viranşehir, and they related an Ottoman reign of terror in Urhoy. The German ambassador reported that the Ottoman Empire was being "cleared" of its indigenous Christians by "elimination." In July 1915, he confirmed that Assyrians from Midyat, Nisibis, and Jazirah had also been slain.[30]

Jevdet Pasha, the governor of Van, is reported to have held a meeting in February 1915 at which he said, "We have cleansed the Armenians and Assyrians from Azerbaijan, and we will do the same in Van."[31] In late 1915, Jevdet Bey, military governor of Van Vilayet, upon entering Siirt (or Seert) with 8000 soldiers whom he deemed "The Butchers' Battalion," ordered the massacre of almost 20,000 Assyrian civilians in at least 30 villages.[32]

On March 3, 1918, the Ottoman army, led by Kurdish soldiers, assassinated one of the most important Assyrian leaders at the time, Mar Benyamin Shimon. Shimon had been the patriarch of the Assyrian Church of the East since he was 14 years old. He had worked to negotiate a truce between the Assyrians and the Kurdish population with Simko Shikak, a Kurdish tribal leader. Simko Shikak was a brigand-turned-leader and prepared a plan to sabotage the negotiations by assassinating the patriarch, forcing the Assyrian population into despondency and desperation. Mar Benyamin Shimon arrived with his guards and advisors. Towards the end of the meeting, Simko and his forces sabotaged the meeting and assassinated Mar Benyamin Shimon and all of his guards except for one man, who managed to escape and

---

[30] Dominik J., Schaller and Jürgen Zimmerer, (2008) "Late Ottoman Genocides: The Dissolution of the   Ottoman Empire and Young Turkish Population and Extermination Policies." Journal of Genocide Research, 10:1, pp. 7–14
[31] Ibid.
[32] D. Gaunt, "The Assyrian Genocide of 1915," Assyrian Genocide Research Center, 2009

disseminate the tragic news.[33]

This event resulted in retaliation by the Assyrians. Malik Yosip Khoshaba led a successful attack against the Ottomans. Assyrian forces in the region also attacked the Kurdish fortress of Simko Shikak, the leader who had assassinated Mar Benyamin Shimon. They successfully stormed it, defeating the Kurds; however, Simko escaped and fled. Several days later, Simko was found and killed.

By the end of the First World War, the Assyrian nation had lost nearly two-thirds of its population, estimated to be around 250,000 Assyrian people. In conjunction with the devastating loss of population and resources, the Assyrian people experienced several transitions of power, as the end of World War I induced the creation of many small states seeking sovereignty, which caused more resentment against Assyrians. With the British mandate over Iraq, the Assyrians sought employment with British petroleum companies and Assyrian levies. The Assyrian levies were organized militia members who were trained to protect the Assyrian people and the British interest in Iraq. Despite the atrocities and hardships suffered by the Assyrians during both World Wars, the Assyrians provided the British and allied powers indispensable support, potential Assyrian autonomy remained undeveloped. The British government did not reciprocate any autonomous land for Assyrian support in the Middle East.

---

[33] Ibid.

The conclusion of the British mandate of Iraq caused considerable unease among the Assyrians, who felt betrayed by the British. The Assyrian leadership, which consisted of the Assyrian Church of the East's patriarch and tribal Maliks stressed that "any treaty with the Iraqis had to take into consideration their desire for an autonomous position similar to the Ottoman millet system."[34] The Iraqi government, on the other hand, felt that the Assyrian demands, when placed alongside the Kurdish disturbances in the north, represented a conspiracy by the British to divide Iraq by agitating its minorities.[35]

After the emergence of Iraqi independence, the new Assyrian spiritual leader Mar Eshai Shimun XXIII, the Catholicos-Patriarch of the Assyrian Church of the East, requested fervently that the Assyrians be given autonomy within Iraq, seeking support from the United Kingdom and pressing his case before the League of Nations in 1932. His followers planned to resign from the Assyrian levies (a military force under the command of the British that served British interests) and to re-group as a militia and concentrate in the north, creating a de facto Assyrian enclave.[36]

In the spring of 1933, Malik Yaqu, a former levies' officer, engaged in a political campaign on behalf of Mar Shimun and the Assyrian interest, persuading the Assyrians not to apply for Iraqi nationality or accept the settlement offered to them by the central government. An estimated 200-armed man accompanied Yaqu. Unfortunately, the Iraqi government's response to the campaign was contrary to the Assyrian cause. Yaqu's campaign was described as an ac

---

[34] K. Husry, (April 1974), "The Assyrian Affair of 1933 (I)," International Journal of Middle East Studies (Cambridge University Press) pp. 161–176
[35] D. Gaunt, J. Bet-Şawoce, (2006), Massacres, resistance, protectors: Muslim-Christian Relations in Eastern Anatolia During World War I, Gorgias Press LLC,
[36] R. Stafford, (2006) [1935], The Tragedy of the Assyrians, Gorgias Press LLC.

act of defiance by the Iraqi authorities. The Iraqi government was concerned about the political activities the Assyrians cultivated, and their concerns caused distress among the Kurds and the Iraqi government. Thus, the Iraqi government, coupled with assistance from Kurdish tribes, began sending its armed forces to the Dohuk region in order to intimidate Yaqu and use coercion to discourage the Assyrians from joining the cause.[37] In June 1933, Mar Shimun was invited to Baghdad for negotiations with Hikmat Sulayman's government and was detained there after refusing to relinquish temporal authority.[38]

He would eventually be exiled to Cyprus and later relocated to the United States. Shortly after the exile of the Assyrian patriarch, Iraqi forces and leadership began a smear campaign against the Assyrian people, informing Iraqi citizens that Assyrian Christians planned to insert poison into an Iraqi waterway and blow up bridges vital for commerce. This false pretense resulted in the Iraqi government justifying a preemptive attack against the Assyrians. During the attacks, Assyrian people were murdered and raped; their villages were burned and destroyed. In 1933, a witness, who spread the news to British newspapers, in which the following was written, brought the violent Assyrian struggle to light:

---

[37] Ibid.
[38] Biography of His Holiness, The Assyrian Martyr, The Late Mar Eshai Shimun XXIII Committee of the 50th Anniversary of the Patriarchate of Mar Eshai Shimun XXIII.

A cold-blooded and methodical massacre of all the men in the village then followed, a massacre which for the black treachery in which it was conceived and the callousness with which it was carried out, was as foul a crime as any in the blood-stained annals of the Middle East. The Assyrians had no fight left in them, partly because of the state of mind to which the events of the past week had reduced them, largely because they were disarmed. Had they been armed it seems certain that Ismail Abawi Tohalla and his bravos would have hesitated to take them on in fair fight. Having disarmed them, they proceeded with the massacre according to plan. This took some time. Not that there was any hurry, for the troops had the whole day ahead of them. Their opponents were helpless and there was no chance of any interference from any quarter whatsoever. Machine gunners set up their guns outside the windows of the houses in which the Assyrians had taken refuge, and having trained them on the terror-stricken wretches in the crowded rooms, fired among them until not a man was left standing in the shambles. In some other instance the blood lust of the troops took a slightly more active form, and men were dragged out and shot or bludgeoned to death and their bodies thrown on a pile of dead.[39]

After the massacre in the town of Simele, Assyrians began to immigrate to Europe, Australia, Asia, and the United States, which has led to an international diaspora for the Assyrian people, causing the Assyrian population to be spread thin in its indigenous regions and villages, which were once inhabited by Assyrians and are now possessed by Kurdish tribes. The Simele massacre inspired Raphael Lemkin to create the concept of genocide.[40]

---

[39] R. Stafford, (2006) [1935], The Tragedy of the Assyrians, Gorgias Press LLC
[40] Raphael Lemkin. "Genocide" Europe World. 22 June 2001.

In 1933, Lemkin made a presentation to the Legal Council of the League of Nations' conference on international criminal law in Madrid, for which he prepared an essay on the crime of barbarity as a crime against international law. The concept of the crime, which later evolved into the idea of genocide, was based on the Simele massacre, the Armenian Genocide, and the Jewish Holocaust.[41]

The massacres also affected the present and future perception of Assyrians in the newly established Kingdom of Iraq. Kanan Makiya argued that "the killing of Assyrians transcended tribal, religious, and ethnic barriers, as Arabs, Kurds, and Yazidis were united in their anti-Assyrian and anti-Western sentiments."[42] According to Makiya, the pogrom was "the first genuine expression of national independence in a former Arab province of the Ottoman Empire," and the killing of Assyrian Christians was seen as a national duty.[43] August 7 officially became Martyrs Day in commemoration of those Assyrians who were systematically killed in 1933; on that day, the Iraqi government unjustifiably killed an estimated 5000 Assyrians.

With all of the recurring massacres and human rights violations throughout the decades against the Assyrian people, the international community has done very little to assist this civilization's indigenous community and to protect their identity. Examples of the international community's neglect against the Assyrian cause is the lack of recognition of the Assyrian Genocide and the massacre of Simele. While there are over 100 documented accounts of the Assyrian Genocide, the Turkish government has not yet recognized its brutal past. Additionally, the United States, England, France, and Russia have not officially recognized the Assyrian Genocide through their elected officials. The only countries to have recognized the Assyrian genocide through its elected representatives are Armenia, The Netherlands, Germany and Sweden.

---

[41] Ibid.
[42] K. Makiya, (1998) [1989], Republic of fear: The politics of modern Iraq. University of California Press.
[43] Ibid.

Despite the vast amount of evidence pointing to the historical reality of the Assyrian Genocide—eyewitness accounts, official archives, photographic evidence, the reports of diplomats, and the testimony of survivors—denial of the Assyrian Genocide by successive regimes in Turkey has persisted from 1915 to the present.

The argument of denial has remained the same: It never happened; Turkey and other groups are not responsible; therefore, the term "genocide" does not apply. The mechanism of denial, however, has shifted over the years. In the period immediately following World War I, the tactic was to place blame on what occurred to be a mere security measure that had "gone awry due to unscrupulous officials, Kurds, and common criminals."[44] This was followed by an attempt to avoid the whole issue, with silence, diplomatic efforts, and political pressure applied where possible.[45] In the 1930s, for example, Turkey pressured the U.S. State Department into preventing MGM Studios from producing a film based on Franz Werfel's The Forty Days of Musa Dagh, a book that depicted aspects of the genocide in a district located west of Antioch on the Mediterranean Sea, far from the Russian front.[46]

In the 1960s, prompted by the worldwide commemoration of the fiftieth anniversary of the genocide, efforts were made to influence journalists, teachers, and public officials by telling "the other side of the story." Foreign scholars were encouraged to revise the record of genocide, presenting an account largely blaming the Assyrians or Armenians or, in another version, "wartime conditions," which claimed the lives of more Turks than Assyrians.[47]

---

[44] http://www.anca.org/genocide/denial.php (accessed May. 2013)
[45] Ibid.
[46] Ibid.
[47] Ibid.

Thereafter, Turkey tried to prohibit any mention of the genocide in a United Nations report and was successful in placing pressure on the Reagan and Bush administrations to overthrow congressional resolutions that would have designated April 24 as a national day of remembrance of the Armenian Genocide, which included information concerning the Assyrian people.

The Turkish government has also attempted to exclude any mention of the genocide from American textbooks. Stronger efforts still have been made to prevent any discussion of the 1915 genocide being formally included in the social studies curriculum as part of Holocaust and genocide studies.

There have also been attempts by the Turkish government to disrupt academic conferences and public discussions of the genocide. A notable example was the attempt by Turkish officials to force cancellation of a conference in Tel Aviv in 1982 if the Armenian/Assyrian Genocide were to be discussed, and this demand was backed up with threats to the safety of the Jews in Turkey.[48] The US Holocaust Memorial Council reported similar threats over plans to include references to the Armenian Genocide within the interpretive framework of the Holocaust Memorial Museum in Washington. At the same time, Turkey has sought to make an absolute distinction between the Holocaust and the Armenian Genocide, designating the latter as "alleged" or "so-called."

---

[48] Ibid.

In sum, the Assyrian Genocide has been overlooked. The lack of recognition of the Assyrian ethnic cleansings of the Great War and beyond assigns Assyrians to an under-inclusive group in an over-inclusive discussed topic of human rights. Rosie Malek Younan, an Assyrian actress, author, and activist, summaries the struggle of the recognition of the Assyrian Genocide in her address to House of Commons in London. "When we perpetually allow the practice of genocide and holocaust and consent to the denial of such actions to linger for decades as in the case of the Assyrians ... we are in essence consenting to denial as a compromise. Denial is not a compromise."[49]

---

[49] Rosie Malek-Yonan. Quotes-Rosie Malek-Yonan. Rosie Malek-Yonan's Official Website (www.RosieMalek-Yonan.com). Web. 12 Mar. 2015.)

SECTION II—EXTERNAL INSTABILITY

CHAPTER FIVE – IRAQ, SYRIA, AND ISIL

Unfortunate circumstances caused Iraq and Syria to become an unstable breeding ground for terrorist. This uncertainty has helped a brutal and irrational terror group, known as the Islamic State of Iraq and the Levant (ISIL). ISIL has placed the Assyrian community in the Middle East in a position of dire need, a move that Assyrians have labeled the "last plight" in their aboriginal region.[50] ISIL's intellectual and sophisticated factions have come from the disenfranchised Sunni Iraqis caused by the corporatist "model" theory effects of the War on Iraq. The invasion of Iraq was sold to the public through fear of weapons of mass destruction.[51] However, an ulterior motive for the invasion was to create a "model" theory for a corporatist state.[52] The model theory is based on cleansing the Middle East of terrorism and converting the region into a "free market democracy." Under this model, "the region was deemed to be a breeding zone for terror."[53] The September 11 hijackers were from "Saudi, Egypt, UAE, and Lebanon; Iran funding Hezbollah; Syria housing Hamas; Iraq sending money to Palestinian suicide bombers."[54] The purpose behind terror was due to a "deficit of free market democracy" overlooking United States foreign policy that induced terror movements.[55]

"The invasion intended not to nation-build but rather to create a new nation, and any residue from the former nation would get in the way of the new corporate development."[56] However, the corporate model theory failed to appreciate Iraqi culture, which dates back to the cradle of civilization, transcending into above-average education with

---

[50] www.thelastplight.com

[51] "Deputy Secretary Wolfowitz Interview with Sam Tannenhaus," Vanity Fair, News Transcript, May 9, 2003, www.defenselink.mil.

[52] Naomi, Klein "16 Erasing Iraq." In The Shock Doctrine: The Rise of Disaster Capitalism, 327. New York, NY: Penguin, 2007.

[53] Ibid.

[54] Ibid.

[55] FOOTNOTE: 2007 Index of Economic Freedom (Washington, DC: Heritage Foundation and The Wall Street Journal, 2007), 326, www.heritage.org.

[56] Thomas L. Friedman, "What Were They Thinking?" New York Times, October 7, 2005.

literacy rates as high as 89 percent.[57] In the new model Iraq, the government played the role of "cash machines equipped for withdrawals and deposits." "Corporations withdrew funds through massive contracts and then repaid the U.S. government—not with reliable work but with campaign contributions and loyal support for the next elections,"[58] while people in Iraq were expected to watch as contractors created an "exclusive economic boom based on easy taxpayer money and relaxed regulations."[59]

Further, Iraqi men were trained militarily and opposed any foreign investment. However, the model theory proceeded by "fighting terror, spreading frontier capitalism, holding elections, and granting freedom for multinationals to feed off a freshly privatized state based on new economic laws."[60] Halliburton, Bechtel, Parsons, KPMG, CH2M Hill, Research Triangle Institute, DynCorp, Vinnell, Carlyle Group-USIS, Creative Associates, Lockheed Martin, Baker Botts, New Bridge Strategies, HSBC, Shell, BP, Exxon Mobile, and others were among the multinationals participating in the reconstruction.[61] The result was that, "after all the layers of corporations had taken their cut, there was next to nothing left for the people performing the reconstruction efforts."[62]

---

[57] Rajiv Chandrasekaran, Imperial Life in the Emerald City: Inside Iraq's Green Zone. FOOTNOTE: World Bank, World Development Report 1990 (Oxford World Bank, 1990), 178-79; New Mexico coalition for literacy, New Mexico Literacy Profile, 2005-2006 Programs, www.nmcl.org.

[58] Ibid.

[59] Naomi Klein "20 Disaster Apartheid." In The Shock Doctrine: the Rise of Disaster Capitalism, 412. New York, NY: Penguin, 2007.

[60] Ibid.

[61] Naomi, Klein "17 Ideological Blowback." In The Shock Doctrine: the Rise of Disaster Capitalism, 346. New York, NY: Penguin, 2007.

[62] Ibid.

The new economic laws enticed foreign investors to take part in the privatization auction to build new factories and retail outlets in Iraq and, according to The Economist, "wish-list that foreign investors and donor agencies dream of for developing markets."[63] Such laws included lowering Iraq's corporate tax rate from 45 percent to 15 percent, privatizing Iraq's national assets allowing foreign companies to own 100 percent of Iraqi assets and permitting companies to take 100 percent of the profits made in Iraq out of the country untaxed.[64] Investors could sign leases and contracts that would last 40 years and then be eligible for renewal, which meant that future elected governments would be encumbered with deals signed by their occupiers.[65] These new laws made it impossible for any groups in Iraq to develop resources that were promised for reconstruction because foreign corporations had the leverage to benefit from the new economic laws without any attachment to the former government's debt.

---

[63] "Let's All Go to the Yard Sale," The Economist, September 27, 2003.
[64] Ibid.
[65] Coalition Provisional Authority, Order Number 37 Tax Strategy for 2003, September 19, 2003, www.iraqcoalition.org; Coalition Provisional Authority, Order Number 39 Foreign Investment, December 20, 2003, www.iraqcoalition.org; Dana Milbank and Walter Pincus, "U.S. Administrator Imposes Flat Tax System on Iraq," Washington Post, November 2, 2003; Rajiv Chandrasekaren, "U.S. Funds for Iraq are Largely Unspent," Washington Post, July 4, 2004. FOOTNOTE: Mark Gregory, "Baghdad's Missing Cash to Iraq. And Watched it Vanish," Guardian (London), February 8, 2007.

Compounding the problem was the Bush Administration's failure to mediate any forgiveness of Iraq's pre-invasion debts under Saddam. James Baker, "special envoy on Iraq's debt, was to erase 90 percent to 95 percent of Iraq's foreign debt. Instead, the debt was merely rescheduled equivalent to 99 percent of the country's GDP."[66] Baker had a conflict of interest: "representing the United States and Carlyle, which was a partner with Kuwait, an Iraqi creditor from the 1991 invasion." Carlyle had a preexisting interest with Kuwait and Baker, which posed a conflict to materially limit and adversely affect the American taxpayer and Iraqi people. In 2005–2006, Iraq made "$2.59 billion in reparation payments for Saddam's war, mostly to Kuwait—resources that were desperately needed to meet Iraqi humanitarian crisis and to rebuild the country."[67]

The model theory was a "public sector reduced to a minimal number of employees, mostly contract workers unfamiliar with Iraq, living in a Halliburton city state, tasked with signing corporate-friendly laws drafted by foreign investors"[68] Handing out "duffle bags of cash to Western contractors protected by mercenary soldiers," themselves "shielded by full legal immunity, thus causing people around the model theory to become furious, and increasing their consciousness to religious fundamentalism because it's the only source of power in a hollowed-out state."[69]

Iraq's only consistent characteristic as a nation after the US-led coalition invasion has been instability. The chaos, violence, and unrest caused by insurgency, collateral damage from war, and historic secretariat conflicts are the main factors involved.

---

[66] David Leigh, "Carlyle Pulls Out of Iraq Debt Recovery Consortium," Guardian (London), October 15, 2004; United Nations Compensation Commission, "payment of Compensation," press releases, 2005- 2006, www.unog.ch; Klein, "James Baker's Double Life"; World Bank, "Data Sheet for Iraq," October 23, 2006, www.worldbank.org.
[67] Ibid.
[68] Ibid.
[69] Naomi Klein "17 Ideological Blowback." In The Shock Doctrine: the Rise of Disaster Capitalism, 341. New York, NY: Penguin, 2007.

These factors have curbed the process of democratization to a counterproductive sequence of events that has pulled America back into the region and has led ethnic native minorities, such as the Assyrians, to be caught between proxy wars, thus contributing to the lack of resources for Assyrian in their native homelands. As a result, it is essential to examine the sequence of events in Iraq that has led to the rise of an unprecedented evil group that has terrorized Iraq and Syria.

Empirically, Iraq is clearly still clearing the residue from the war and sectarian factions rather than proceeding with an effective democracy. The following is a detailed chronology of the events that occurred up to March 1, 2011. The chronology was produced by PBS's Frontline documentary series, "Losing Iraq."

April 2003

In April 2003, a 39-foot stone statue, entitled Sahat al-Firdaus Square, was erected in an open public space in Baghdad to commemorate Sadaam Hussein's 65th birthday. A year later, American forces "helped tear down the same statue along with eager Iraqi citizens who were determined to make a statement in alignment with the destruction of the statue to symbolize the destruction of Saddam Hussein's regime and a potential democratic future in Iraq."[70] Subsequently, following the toppling of the statue, the same Iraqi citizens began weeks of looting former presidential palaces and ministry defense buildings.[71]

Despite the obvious unrest among the citizens, the Bush administration began to entertain ideas facilitating the U.S. removal from the region, even though the potential for unrest was ripening toward chaos. Then General Tommy Franks and Secretary of Defense, Donald Rumsfeld administered removal war plans.[72]

---

[70] David Zucchino (July 3, 2004). "Army Stage-Managed Fall of Hussein Statue." Los Angeles Times (Common Dreams). Archived from the original on July 5, 2004
[71] "Losing Iraq," July 29, 2014, Frontline Documentary
[72] Ibid.

As tensions rose, General Franks provided guidance on the ground that his commanders should be prepared to withdraw all American forces except for a division of an estimated 110,000 troops, and a division of 35,000 soldiers that would oversee Iraq.[73] However, General Jack Keane stated that the plan did not have adequate security for the country because it failed to factor in the possibility of an uprising by insurgents as a response to withdrawal.[74]

May 2003

On May 1, 2003, President George W. Bush claimed that the major combat operations ended with a banner created by White House Staff that stated, "Mission accomplished." Although President Bush had proclaimed that there was still work to do in dangerous regions in Iraq, the Bush Administration claimed that Iraq was "free."[75]

The administration's strategy was to pull the troops out of Iraq and hand over authority to a United States citizen. The duty to appoint the citizen was assigned to Vice President Dick Cheney, who delegated the authority to Scooter Libby, the VP chief of staff to Dick Cheney and Paul Wolfowitz, the deputy secretary of defense. Wolfowitz and Libby selected Paul J. Bremer, III, a close friend and confidante to Scooter Libby.[76]

Bremer was a former businessman, a diplomat who was a managing director for Henry Kissinger. Despite Bremer's ambassadorial experience with Kissinger, he had no prior knowledge of the Middle East, did not speak Arabic, and had no information concerning the region. Coincidentally, Bremer had no practical experience with Middle Eastern politics. After a two-week crash course about Middle Eastern politics, Bremer was sent to Baghdad to oversee a coalition of Americans called the Coalition Provisional Authority (CPA).

---

[73] Ibid.

[74] Interview with General Jack Kean. "Losing Iraq," July 29, 2014, Frontline Documentary

[75] Text of Bush's Speech." CBS News. May 1, 2003. Archived from the original on May 1, 2006.

[76] "Losing Iraq," July 29, 2014, Frontline Documentary

June–August 2003

As Bremer drove into Baghdad to serve as an ambassador for the Bush administration, he was shocked by the lack of government services in place in Iraq. Baghdad's infrastructure had been devastated by looting, fires, and sewage problems. Bremer settled into the Green Zone, an isolated city heavily fortified by coalition forces. Within this headquarters, Bremer administered his plan to assume authority in Iraq.[77]

Bremer's decisions were based on the questionable assumption that democratic stability is possible while surrounded by contentious divisions within Iraq. Saddam Hussein's' Ba'ath Party was dominated by Sunni rule. Hussein's regime dictated brutally over factions such as the majority of the Shi'a Muslims, Kurdish, Yiezidis, and Assyrians. Therefore, one of Bremer's plans was to remove Hussein's agents and loyalists for replacements consisting of Shia and Kurds to work together in a collegial manner.

Within days of his arrival in Baghdad, Bremer issued two controversial orders: disband the Iraqi National Army and remove those with membership in Hussein's Ba'ath Party from professional positions. Advisers were concerned that the orders would alienate any skilled Sunnis who were willing to participate in the new government.

De-Ba'athification

The first action implemented by Bremer was the de-Ba'athification of the Iraqi government. The order was to remove any former Ba'ath party members from actively participating in the democratization of the new Iraqi government. The effect created a climate in which "people who had no tie to the senior structure were expelled from democratic participation in the Iraqi government."[78]

---

[77] Ibid.
[78] CPA Order number 1 Dissolution of Entities Iraq Coalition.org. Accessed 2015-03-03.

In an interview featured in PBS's Frontline documentary series, Lt. Gen. Jay Garner, who briefly led the reconstruction effort after the invasion, stated that he and the former CIA station chief in Baghdad warned Bremer specifically that "the de-Ba'athification order would oust 30,000 to 50,000 capable Sunni professionals from the government, leaving them disenfranchised, angry, and likely to become recruits for the nascent insurgency."

In sum, the de-Ba'athification of the Iraqi government would be counterproductive because the Sunnis had run the government for 20 years, and discriminating against Sunnis and their representation in a newly democratized Iraq would produce even more insurgence than otherwise.

Disbanding the Iraqi Military

Another decision ordered by the CPA through Bremer was the dissolution of the military of Iraq. In response, 100,000 disgruntled men took their weapons home and began making plans to form a group opposing the occupation in Iraq. Those who were expelled from their professional administrative positions were now in joint dissatisfaction with former military personnel, officers, and soldiers.[79]

Three days after Bremer made the order to disband the military, the first major attack on the airport road took place in Iraq. By August, two major bombings in Baghdad occurred at the Jordanian embassy and the United Nations headquarters. This effect caused Iraq to face looting and opposition with grenades and weapons, thus triggering an insurgency. For example, on August 7, 2003 insurgency groups committed dozens of insurgency attacks, coupled with the beheadings of seven non-Iraqi hostages. By the summer of 2003, the White House had a new plan: "get out." The military retreated inside large, fortified bases. Politically, U.S. officials focused on their exit strategy to establish a constitution, set up a governing council, and leave the Iraqis to govern Iraq.

June 2004: American transfers sovereignty to Iraqi government

---

[79] CPA Order number 2 Dissolution of Entities Iraq Coalition.org. Accessed 2015-03-03.

On June 28, 2004, Bremer handed over authority to the interim Iraqi Governing Council. But his departure was hardly triumphant; the move came two days ahead of schedule because of fears of an insurgency attack.[80]

February 2006: Shiite and Sunni Conflict Erupts Into Civil War

Until February 22, 2006, Iraq's Shiite majority had largely tolerated a series of attacks by the Sunni insurgents. But Sunni insurgents, eager to provoke a sectarian war, pushed Shiite leaders over the edge when insurgents destroyed Al-Askari Mosque in Samarra, one of Shiite Islam's holiest sites.[81]

Over the next 10 days, Shiite militias took their revenge, massacring Sunnis. In Baghdad, their death squads moved house-to-house, killing as they went. Furthermore, Shiite arsonists set a Sunni mosque ablaze in the neighborhood of Bayaa in western Baghdad.[82]

Thus, Iraq became the site of a "blood bath, with hundreds of people being killed every day and thousands a week"; the government was "fractured, heading toward a failed state, with no services, no work, and no market; the people were in survival mode; and the entire state of Iraq was in jeopardy, while the United States was about to suffer humiliating defeat."[83]

May 2006–January 2007: The US seeks a new plan to help subdue the bloodshed

---

[80] Interview with Paul J. Bremer, "Losing Iraq," Frontline Documentary.
[81] Ellen Knickmeyer (February 23, 2006). "Bombing Shatters Mosque in Iraq." The Washington Post. Archived from the original on February 21, 2011. Retrieved February 23, 2006.
[82] Larry Kaplow (13 June 2007). "Attacked Again." Newsweek. Retrieved 15 June 2007.
[83] Interview with Ryan Crocker US Ambassador "Losing Iraq," Frontline Documentary.

President Bush determined that the US needed a new strategy to quell the bloodshed. That included a new partner in the Iraqi leadership—someone who could rally the Shia but also not be perceived as too sectarian by the Sunnis and Kurds. Nouri al-Maliki, a minor figure in the Iraqi parliament, emerged as a potential favorite among US officials, despite his lack of experience.[84]

The US also needed a new approach on the ground. This attempt was "a last-ditch effort to salvage the American incursion in Iraq. Bush brought in General David Petraeus to lead what became known as the surge—an additional 30,000 US troops who moved off the large, fortified bases and into the neighborhoods. Petraeus was trained in counterinsurgency and developed a plan that would attempt to persuade Sunnis in their neighborhoods to battle against Sunni insurgents for monetary gain.

President Bush described the surge as a means to create a "unified, democratic federal Iraq that can govern itself, defend itself, and sustain itself, and is an ally in the War on Terror."[85] The strategy was to change the focus for the US military "to help Iraqis clear and secure neighborhoods, to help them protect the local population, and to help ensure that the Iraqi forces left behind are capable of providing security."[86]

U.S. forces sustained their heaviest losses during this period. But, in August, they caught a break: Muqtada al-Sadr, the head of a powerful Shia militia, called for a ceasefire and stopped attacking coalition forces. The move created a lull in the violence, thus allowing US forces to focus on the Sunni insurgency.[87]

2008: Bush's Final Decision in Iraq as Commander and Chief

---

[84] "Losing Iraq" Frontline Documentary
[85] President George W. Bush (January 10, 2007). "President's Address to the Nation." Office of the Press Secretary.
[86] Ibid.
[87] "Losing Iraq," Frontline Documentary

The confluence of three factors—the surge, the "Awakening," and Sadr's ceasefire— reduced the violence in Iraq to a low-grade insurgency. Hoping to maintain that progress, President Bush signed an agreement with Prime Minster Maliki before he left office that would ensure that American troops would remain in Iraq through 2011.

2009–2011: Barack Obama is now president and plans a removal date of the troops

As he campaigned for the presidency, Barack Obama promised war-weary Americans that he would withdraw US forces from Iraq. Within his first month in office, the new president set a pullout date: December 2011.[88]

With the advice of the Pentagon and others, the president considered keeping a small troop presence in the country. But both the U.S. and Iraqi governments were unable to reach an agreement on the size or the legal guidelines under which they would remain. By December 2011, almost all U.S. forces had left Iraq. The U.S. diplomatic effort was also scaled back, leaving Maliki to govern on his own.[89]

Islamic State and Levant (ISIL)

It is important to note that ISIL's rise to a terror network was a process that began in 1999 in Jordan and exacerbated by the unintended circumstances of the Iraq War and civil war in Syria. For half a decade, ISIL operated under different identities and labels: Jamaat al Twhid wasl-Jihad, followed by Tanzim Qaidat al-Jihad fi Bilad al-Rafidayn, otherwise known as al- Qaeda in Iraq. They then labeled themselves as ISIL in 2006 and reiterated the name change during ISIL's rise from 2011 to 2014.

---

[88] "Obama's Speech on Iraq" Council on Foreign Relations March 19 2008 retrieved March 3, 2015
[89] "Losing Iraq" Frontline Documentary

According to the Washington Institute of Near East Policy, ISIL was created by Abu Musab al-Zarqarwi in 1999 as a reaction to the jihadist movement against the Soviet Union in Afghanistan in the 1980s. Al-Zarqarwi called the organization Jamaat al-Tawhid wasl-Jihad (JTWJ).[90] JTWJ was created with the particular intention to overthrow the Kingdom of Jordan, toppling the monarchy, and further toppling other monarchies and dictatorships to help establish a "Levant," which is typical reference to a period of ancient or archaic history.[91]

Al-Zarqawi interpreted a monarch as un-Islamic, according to Sunni Islamic Jurisprudence. Furthermore, JTWJ attempted to establish a caliphate based on the motivating factor of the creation of the State of Israel, the United States occupation of Iraq, and the humiliation of the Arab nation.[92]

During its processing in 1999, JTWJ received funding from Osama bin Laden's al-Qaeda, which continued for two years. Despite this arrangement, there were ideological differences between bin Laden and Al-Zaraqarwi concerning the killing of Shiite Muslims. The group would be trained, educated, and mobilized, and its members planned and committed attacks that included the assassination of United States diplomat Laurence Foley in 2002.[93]

Subsequently, after the U.S.-led coalition invaded Iraq, with an outlet caused by Bremer's de-Ba'athification and the disbanding of Iraqi armed services, JTWJ was able to expand its network for the purpose of presenting a systematic and continuous resistance to the U.S.-led coalition. This resistance was the primary focus against the CPA implemented by the Bush administration. From August 7, 2003, to December 3, 2004, JTWJ committed dozens of insurgency attacks, coupled with the beheadings of seven non-Iraqi hostages.

2011–2014: ISIL's Rise

[90] Washington Institute for Near East Policy. June 2014. Retrieved 14 February 2015.
[91] Ibid.
[92] Ibid.
[93] Jeffery Pool, (18 October 2004). "Zarqawi's pledge of allegiance to al-Qaeda." Jamestown Foundation. Retrieved 16 September 2014.

In response to President Barack Obama's pull-out date of December 31, 2011, American troops left Iraq.[94] The day after American troops left, Al Maliki issued an arrest warrant for the Sunni vice president, Tariq al-Hashimi, forcing him to flee the country. Al Maliki then pushed other prominent Sunnis from political office and the military and ultimately stopped payments to the Sons of Iraq.[95]

Consequently, those Sunnis who participated in the coalition forces in 2007 would now be in opposition to the Iraqi national government and sought to seek joint commitment to the resistance with the insurgency they were initially ordered to fight. In other words, the message was clear: there would be no role for Sunnis in Al Maliki's Shia regime. For many Sunnis, their only recourse would be to join the fight against Al Maliki's regime.

In 2014, disenfranchised Sunnis found an outlet as a militant group that had recently coalesced in the fight against President Bashar al-Assad in Syria. The militant group, which had a reputation of ruthlessness, gained a rapid foothold in Iraq, capturing the towns of Fallujah and Ramadi in January and Iraq's second-largest city, Mosul, in June 2014. ISIL was able to siege a city of 1.3 million people with 800 militant fighters, a spectacular offensive that humiliated the Iraqi government in a city that many people had given their lives to protect.

---

[94] "Last US troops leave Iraq, ending war." USA Today. 17 December 2011. Retrieved 18 December 2011.
[95] "Losing Iraq" Frontline Documentary.

During the June attacks and siege of Mosul, the Iraqi National Army abandoned its posts, tasks, and duties as members of a common defense. Thus, innocent civilians, such as the Assyrians and Yezidis, were forced to leave their residences and seek refuge in uninhabitable regions of Iraq. Furthermore, major landmarks like the Mosul Dam were now controlled by ISIL in Mosul. As a result of ISIL's momentum, the Obama Administration urged Prime Minster Malaki to step down in the midst of the chaotic turmoil. On August 13, 2014, Al-Malaki stepped down as prime minister to "safeguard the high interests of the country." Maliki was replaced by Haider al-Abadi. The Obama Administration welcomed the transition, labeling the change as a "step forward" in uniting Iraq.

Financing ISIL

ISIL as an organization is dubious in many forms. It is difficult to "ascertain what motivates the decision-making process concerning the group."[96] The only evident understanding of ISIL is its brutality and allegiance to an archaic fundamental worldview of establishing an Islamic caliphate, an Islamic state led by a group of religious authorities under a supreme leader—the Caliph—who is believed to be the successor to Muhammad. Despite its archaic worldview, ISIL has managed to accumulate wealth in an unprecedented form.[97]

ISIL's momentum and progress toward achieving its goals as a caliphate has been supplemented by numerous methods of financing. In 2014, the RAND Corporation carried out a study of 200 documents—personal letters, expense reports, and membership rosters—that had been gathered from Islamic State of Iraq (al-Qaeda in Iraq).[98] It is purported that, from 2005 until 2010, outside donations amounted to only 5 percent of the group's operating budgets, with the rest being raised within Iraq.[99] During the time period studied, cells were required to send up to 20 percent of the income generated from kidnapping, extortion rackets, and other activities to the next level of

---

[96] Ibid.
[97] Ibid.
[98] Hannah Allam (23 June 2014). "Records show how Iraqi extremists withstood US anti-terror efforts." McClatchy News. Retrieved 25 June 2014.
[99] Ibid.

the group's leadership.

Higher-ranking commanders would then redistribute the funds to provincial or local cells that needed money to conduct attacks.[100] The records show that ISIL was dependent on members of Mosul for cash, which the leadership used to provide additional funds to struggling ISIL cells in Diyala, Salahuddin, and Baghdad.[101]

In mid-2014, Iraqi intelligence obtained information from an ISIL operator, who discovered that the organization had assets worth close to $2 billion,[102] making it the richest jihadist group in the world.[103] About three-quarters of this sum is said to be represented by assets seized after the group captured Mosul in June 2014; this includes possibly up to US$429 million looted from Mosul's central bank, along with additional millions and a large quantity of gold bullion stolen from a number of other banks in Mosul.[104] However, skepticism arose regarding whether ISIL was able to salvage anywhere near that sum from the central bank[105] and even about whether the bank robberies had actually occurred.[106]

---

[100] Ibid.

[101] Ibid.

[102] Martin Chulov (15 June 2014). "How an arrest in Iraq revealed Isis's $2bn jihadist network." The Guardian. Retrieved 17 June 2014.

[103] Jack Moore (11 June 2014). "Mosul Seized: Jihadis Loot $429m from City's Central Bank to Make Isis World's Richest Terror Force." International Business Times UK. Retrieved 19 June 2014.

[104] Terrence McCoy (12 June 2014). "ISIS just stole $425 million, Iraqi governor says, and became the 'world's richest terrorist group.'" The Washington Post. Retrieved 18 June 2014.

[105] "US Official Doubts ISIS Mosul Bank Heist Windfall." NBC News. 24 June 2014. Retrieved 22 July 2014.

[106] Ibid.

The oil exports from oilfields captured by ISIL bring in tens of millions of dollars.[107] One U.S. Treasury official has estimated that ISIL earns $1 million a day from the export of oil. Much of the oil is sold illegally in Turkey.[108] Dubai-based energy analysts have estimated the combined oil revenue from ISIL's Iraqi- Syrian production as high as US$3 million per day.[109] ISIL also extracts wealth through taxation and extortion against Christians and minorities.[110]

The majority of the group's funding derived from the production and sale of energy. It controls around 300 oil wells in Iraq alone. At its peak, it operated 350 oil wells in Iraq but lost 45 to foreign airstrikes.[111] ISIL has captured 60 percent of Syria's total production capacity, and about one fifth of the total capacity is in operation. ISIL earned $2.5 million a day by selling 50,000– 60,000 barrels of oil daily.[112]

Foreign sales rely on a longstanding black market to export via Turkey. Many of the smugglers and corrupt Turkish border guards who helped Saddam Hussein to evade sanctions are helping ISIL to export oil and import cash.[113] Sales include selling electric power from captured power plants in northern Syria; some of this electricity is reportedly sold back to the Syrian government.[114]

Administrators of ISIL

---

[107] Charles C. Caris; Samuel Reynolds (July 2014). "ISIS Governance in Syria." Institute for the Study of War.

[108] Janine di Giovanni; Leah McGrath Goodman; Damien Sharkov (6 November 2014). "How Does ISIS Fund Its Reign of Terror?" Newsweek.

[109] Karen Leigh (2 August 2014). "ISIS Makes Up To $3 Million a Day Selling Oil, Say Analysts." ABC news. Retrieved 8 October 2014.

[110] Scott Bronstein; Drew Griffin (7 October 2014). "Self-Funded and Deep-Rooted: How ISIS Makes its Millions." CNN.

[111] Ibid.

[112] Ibid.

[113] Erika Solomon (28 April 2014). "Syria's Jihadist Groups Fight for Control of Eastern Oilfields." Financial Times. Retrieved 17 June 2014.

[114] Max Fisher (12 June 2014). "How ISIS Is Exploiting the Economics of Syria's Civil War." Vox. Retrieved 17 June 2014.

The Islamic State's activity as a terror group is distinct from any terrorist organization that has operated in the Middle East. Its activities must be planned secretly to shield its leaders while the effect of their strategies must be acknowledged by many to create alertness. Many of ISIL's leaders are focused on protecting its force but are concurrently applying policies based on Shaira Law. Therefore, the group must covertly govern the provinces they seized. They do so by ordering executions, and meticulously planning both offensive and defensive military campaigns.

The patterns of ISIL leadership have proven two important factors, as discussed earlier. First, most of ISIL's influential figures are Iraqi Sunnis, many of whom were once Saddam Hussein loyalists, and several had been detained by the U.S. military camps during the U.S. occupation in Iraq.[115] Second, ISIL is comprised of three main management separations: the caliph, Sharu council, and the Sharia council.

The caliph is the supreme leader of the organizations. The Sharu council is the governing authority, with an estimated seven to 10 members who had ties to the Ba'ath Party. Finally, the Sharia council, which is the most powerful body of the powers, interprets law and ensures either that citizens comply or be punished; the caliph and the Sharia council directly oversee the Sharu council.[116]

The councils have the authority to govern the laws of the province, conducting military campaigns, security and intelligence, religious affairs, finances, and media. Each area is delegated to a senior ISIL member based on his merit; for example, the notable official regarding security and intelligence named Abu Safwan al-Rifai is another former Ba'ath party member and Sunni.[117] All in all, ISIL adopted the characteristics of a state, which has severe effects on the region.

Effect of ISIL

---

[115] Ibid.
[116] Ibid.
[117] Ibid.

ISIL was able to mobilize and accumulate financial resources through its illegal activities because of the instability in the region, lack of an effective war plan, inexperienced administrators of the CPA, and inconsistent support by the occupational coalition, and Iraq's former Prime Minister Malaki's discrimination against Sunnis, which caused more Sunnis to join ISIL. These factors managed to accelerate the mobilization of the group faster than Western leaders expected. Thus, the world was surprised by how quickly the Iraqi army decreased to a small force of fighters. Shia militias have stepped in to fill the void, and sectarian killings are on the rise again, causing President Obama to send 400 United States military advisors and supplemental ground troops in Iraq to counsel the Iraqi military on how to alleviate ISIL's threats to the region.

In August 2014, the United States assembled a coalition of partner countries to combat ISIL. Various countries contributed aircraft, military aid to local ground forces, military advisors to train local forces in country, and bases for operations and training of local ground forces.[118]

In addition to military efforts, many countries mounted a considerable humanitarian effort to assist ethnic minorities in northern Iraq, who are under the threat of genocide or had fled from ISIL in northern Iraq and other areas.[119] In August, in reference to the U.S. involvement in Iraq, President Barack Obama said, "this is going to be a long-term project."[120]

---

[118] "Jordan carries out air strikes in Iraq, killing 55 IS militants." i24 News. i24 News. 4 February 2015. Retrieved 4 February 2015.

[119] RAF jets sent on Iraqi combat mission." BBC News. 27 September 2014. Retrieved 21 October 2014.

[120] "US airstrikes on militants in Iraq." The New York Times. 10 August 2014.

Subsequently, the world's scope is focused on the Middle East and ISIL's threats to the world, as the United Nations, the European Union, United States, Britain, India, Egypt, and Malaysia have all labeled ISIL a terrorist group. Conversely, as the world watches ISIL commit their terrorist attacks, a minimal amount of information and knowledge is accurately disseminated to the public at large. Furthermore, ethnic minority groups such as the Assyrians live in dire need because of limited resources, and reconstruction of a destroyed infrastructure autonomous region.

In June 2011, Syria's civil war escalated into a conflict that poured over its effects to neighboring countries such as Turkey, Jordan, and Iraq. The Syrian Civil War began as a pro- democracy uprising stemming from the torture killings of three teenage boys who graffiti painted an anti-government slogan. Rebel brigades were formed to battle government forces for control of cities, towns, and the countryside. Fighting reached the capital, Damascus, and Aleppo in 2012.[121]

By June 2013, the UN said 90,000 people had been killed in the conflict. However, by August 2014, that figure had more than doubled to 191,000.[122] As a result, more than 3 million people have fled Syria since the start of the conflict, most of them women and children.[123]

The conflict is now more than just a battle between those for or against President Assad. It has acquired sectarian overtones, pitching the country's Sunni majority against the president's Shia Alawite sect, and has drawn in bordering countries and external powers. The armed rebellion has evolved significantly since its establishment, with as many as 1000 groups commanding an estimated 100,000 fighters. Secular moderates are now outnumbered by Islamists and jihadists, whose brutal tactics have caused widespread concern and triggered rebel infighting.[124]

---

[121] BBC - Middle East News. 8 Dec. 2014. Web. 7 Mar. 2015.
[122] Ibid.
[123] Ibid.
[124] Ibid.

Capitalizing on the chaos in the region, ISIL has taken control of huge swathes of territory across Iraq and Syria. Its many foreign fighters in Syria are now involved in a "war within a war," battling rebels who object to their tactics as well as Kurdish forces.[125]

By late June 2014, Iraq had lost control of its border with Jordan and Syria.[126] The then prime minister of Iraq Nouri al-Maliki called for a national state of emergency on June 10 following the attack on Mosul, which had been seized overnight by ISIL. However, despite the security crisis, Iraq's parliament did not allow Maliki to declare a state of emergency; many Sunni Arab and ethnic Kurdish legislators boycotted the session because they opposed expanding the prime minister's powers.[127]

As a result of the fall of Mosul, ISIL demanded that Assyrian Christians in the city convert to Islam, pay tribute, or face execution. Subsequently, after ISIL's demands, the Assyrian population was forced to make a mass exodus from Mosul, marking the end of the 1600 years of Assyrian presence in the city.[128] More than 800,000 members of Iraq's religious and ethnic minorities have been driven out of their homes leaving their personal belongings and culture behind.

ISIL has carried out "war crimes including mass killings and abductions as part of a systematic targeting of non-Sunnis and non-Arabs in the north of the country." Survivors of massacres told Amnesty International that, in the northern Sinjar region, scores of men and boys from Iraq's Yazidi minority, some as young as 12, were rounded up, taken to the outskirts of villages, and shot dead by Islamic State militants.[129]

---

[125] Ibid.

[126] Laura Spark-Smith. "More than 100,000 Iraqis have fled their homes." CNN. June 21 2014

[127] Michael Pizzi "Obama's Iraq dilemma." Al Jazera News. June 13, 2014.

[128] "Iraqi Christian church burnings confirmed by EU delegation." Iraq news, the latest Iraq news.

[129] Amnesty International. "Ethnic Cleansing on a Historical Scale." September 2, 2014

"The massacres and abductions being carried out by the Islamic State provide harrowing new evidence that a wave of ethnic cleansing against minorities is sweeping across northern Iraq," said Donatella Rovera, Amnesty's senior crisis response adviser. "The Islamic State is carrying out despicable crimes and has transformed rural areas of Sinjar into blood-soaked killing fields in its brutal campaign to obliterate all traces of non-Arabs and non-Sunni Muslims."[130]

Minorities targeted by the militants include Yazidis, Assyrian Christians, Shiite Turkmen, Shabak, Kakais, and Sabean Mandaeans, all of whom have lived together in northern Iraq for hundreds of years. ISIL seized a large portion of the region in the northern offensive in June and then commandeered the territory, which had been held by Iraqi Kurdish forces in early August.

As noted earlier, the civil war in Syria has played an essential role in the obliteration of the Iraq and Syria border because ISIL has merged its fight for a caliphate to neighboring Syria against the Syrian president.

On February 23, 2015, ISIL's militant group kidnapped more than 200 Assyrians from their homes in northeastern Syria. During the week of February 23, 2015, ISIL attacked 35 Assyrian villages.[131] The hostages mostly consisted of the elderly, women, and children. According to the Syrian Observatory of Human Rights, a United Kingdom monitoring group, the children of the families were caged collectively and held hostage as Assyrian activists pleaded to spare the lives of the innocent civilians. Independence for Assyrians and other minority groups infers freedom from persecution on any basis, whether it is based on ethnicity, nationality, culture, or religion. Furthermore, independence entails the ability to exercise Assyrian culture in their indigenous homeland. Since the 2003 war in Iraq, Assyrians and their yearning for independence has been substantially obstructed by systematic and continuous attacks upon the Assyrian people.

---

[130] Ibid.
[131] Meredith Hoffman. "Islamic States Releases Small Group After Mass Kidnapping." Vice News. March 1, 2015.

CHAPTER SIX – OVER A DECADE OF PERSECUTION (2003-2018)

In 2003, the Assyrian cause was overshadowed by the war in Iraq and the United States- led coalition invasion. After Saddam Hussein's dictatorship was defeated, the process of democratization began in Iraq. From 2003 to 2010, the democratization process precluded any attempt for Assyrians to regain a protected, autonomous region. Since the invasion of Iraq, the Assyrians have been targeted, with at least one-third being cleansed from Iraq and an even greater percentage displaced internally. On September 24, 2008, the government of Iraq passed the new elections law for governorates and local councils. A critical article, popularly known as "Article 50," would have ensured minority representation, but it was "stripped from the legislation despite prior approval."[132]

On October 6, 2008, attacks began on Mosul's Christian Assyrians. "Unknown terrorists came into the auto spare parts shop owned and operated by Ziad Kamal, a 25-year-old paraplegic." Ziad was the sole income earner for his family. His shop was in the Al-Karama district of Mosul; his family was sent away to the town of Bartillah on the Nineveh Plain for safety.[133] Terrorists entered his shop and riddled his body with bullets.

Evan Enwiya, 15 years old, was found dead in October 2008 near his home, which was proximate to the Al-Zahraa Mosque in the Al-Tahrir district of Mosul. Thomas Joseph, a blacksmith in his forties, was killed in his shop on October 4, 2008, in the Al-Sarai Gate district. Amjad Putros and his son Hasam Putros were murdered on October 7, 2008, in the Al-Sukar district of Mosul. Both father and son had worked together in construction and, at the time, were working in someone's home. Extremists entered the home looking for the father and son, with deliberation and intent to commit murder. Both were

---

[132] Iraq Democracy Project. Policy Briefing. October 13, 2008.
[133] Ibid.

executed, while the owners of the home were left unharmed.[134] In Mosul, victims' families are unable to bury the dead because the churches were forced to close. The targeting of students means that even more families are fleeing to safety on the Nineveh Plain rather than proceeding toward education. Within the Nineveh Plain, large towns such as Al-Qosh have issued public declarations of citizens opening their homes to internally displaced families to prevent further flight from Iraq itself. These actions reflected the state of desperation being felt by this vulnerable and targeted minority.[135]

On October 10, 2008, the mayor of the Telkaif district of the Nineveh Plain, Bassim Bello, speaking on public radio about the ethnic cleansing in Mosul, described it as a "horrific campaign of murder and cleansing of more than 12 people in one week." Checkpoints established in Mosul are being used to identify Christians for execution.[136] The singular focus on indigenous Assyrians confirms the methodical targeting of the Assyrian community. The persecution of Assyrian Christian has been continuous in districts such as Dora in Baghdad in 2006 and 2007 and in Basra, a thriving Christian population of well over 250,000 is almost completely displaced.[137]

---

[134] Michael Youash. "The Tipping Point." Iraqi Sustainable Democracy Project. October 2010.
[135] Ibid.
[136] Iraq Democracy Project. Policy Briefing. October 13, 2008
[137] Ibid.

On October 8, 2008, in the Al-Sukar district, a vehicle drove through this residential district the entire day, announcing through a megaphone to Christian residents: "Leave your homes or be killed." Within one 24-hour period, 1165 families were reported to have fled Mosul. Refugee statistics for Iraq from the U.N. High Commissioner for Refugees from as far back as 2007 indicate that Assyrians consistently constitute 17 to 22 percent of refugees. For 2006, the Department of State's International Religious Freedom Report identified no less than 200,000 non-Muslims as refugees and internally displaced persons (IDPs). Extrapolating from this reality and using the data from various humanitarian organizations, one arrives at a modest figure of Roughly between 200,000–400,000 Christian Assyrian refugees.[138]

In 2010, violence against the Assyrian Iraqis remained at a high level. Assyrians endured the second-highest number of murders of Assyrians since the beginning of the war. Some 87 Assyrians were killed from January to December 2010 in robberies, bomb attacks, and kidnappings. Most single incidents of violence happened in Mosul. Because of the Sayidat al- Nejat (Our Lady of Deliverance) cathedral attack, the highest death toll of 54 Assyrians was registered in Baghdad, with a spike of violence in the last months of 2010.[139]

---

[138] Michael Youash. "The Tipping Point." Iraqi Sustainable Democracy Project. October 2010
[139] Ibid.

The majority of the victims were men. Men are targeted on the assumption that gender roles of a father would likely cause the rest of the family to flee or to starve. The attackers want Assyrians to relinquish their future in Iraq and to leave the country in order to minimize their role in the future political landscape of their homeland. Threats and targeted bombings of Assyrians in 2010 produced two major waves of displacement in March and October, from Mosul and Baghdad to northern Iraq and abroad. However, the attack of October 31 on the Sayidat al-Nejat church marked the beginning of a more systematic campaign of violence against Christians.[140] traced back to the high death toll of the Baghdad church attack,[141] approximately 54 percent of the victims died in a church or a church-related attack.[142]

As of 2015, Assyrians continue to face grave threats. According to monitors of the International Organization for Migration (IOM) in Baghdad, security measures have been increased accordingly, including the creation of security checkpoints near the homes of Assyrians in Baghdad. Furthermore, several leaders are in contact with Iraqi security forces for assistance in protecting their communities. However, not even security checkpoints are reliable instruments for providing protection. Many Assyrians intend to move or emigrate. The will to settle down somewhere else is reinforced by rumors in Baghdad of impending violence against Assyrians. This makes Assyrians unable to sell their property for resources before they are forced to flee.[143]

---

[140] IOM. "IOM Emergency needs assessments – Displacement of Christians to the North of Iraq," 15 December 2010.
[141] Ibid.
[142] Ibid.
[143] IOM, "IOM Emergency needs assessments – Displacement of Christians to the North of Iraq," January 2011.

The United Nations High Commissioner for Refugees' (UNHCR) figures on refugees outside the country and internally displaced persons are from March 2010. The UNHCR reported 223,000 active refugee cases for Iraqis living outside Iraq and estimated that approximately 1.8 million Iraqis had fled and remain outside the country. Some 13 percent of all Iraqi refugees registered in Syria, Jordan, Lebanon, Turkey, and Egypt are Assyrian Christians. According to the Assyrian International News Agency (AINA), up to 40 percent of the Iraqi refugees in Jordan and Syria are of Assyrian origin.[144] Internally displaced persons inside Iraq are estimated to number 2.8 million, of which 5 percent are Christians.

Assyrians fleeing from Baghdad face many challenges during their period of refuge. Some of those challenges include employment, shelter, and lack of education. Rental prices for accommodation in the northern region have risen 200 to 300 percent since the exodus of November 2010.[145] Many live with host families and relatives in overcrowded homes. Children are particularly vulnerable after the trauma of displacement because they are often unable to continue their education due to language barriers or difficulties registering in new schools.[146] Many university students have stayed in Baghdad and Mosul in order to complete their exams, having found it difficult to continue their studies in their location of displacement.

Gender-based violence continues to be a serious problem for Assyrian women and girls in Iraq and Syria. Minority Groups International states, "Minority women and children represent the most vulnerable section of Iraqi society."[147] Women remain at risk of attack from extremists. The German Syriac Orthodox nun Sister Hatune, who has been helping victims of violence in Iraq and in the refugee camps in Syria and Jordan since 2005, reports a significant number of actual rapes as well as verbal and physical sexual harassment in public.[148]

---

[144] Assyrian International News Agency. "Assyrians in Tehran Demonstrate Against Baghdad Church Massacre," 17 November 2010.
[145] Ibid.
[146] Ibid.
[147] Lalani Muntaz, "Still Targeted: Continued Persecution of Iraq's Minorities," Minority Rights Group International, June 2010
[148] Ibid.

Depression and despair are common, especially among those who have chosen not to leave their homes because of fear. In particular, women in refugee camps are vulnerable to trafficking and sexual exploitation or forced prostitution due to financial hardship. Evidence presented in this report reveals that ongoing threats restrict Christian women's right to express their particular religious and ethnic identity through the way in which they dress. Not wearing the hijab and the Western-style clothing adds to their visibility as Christians and, thus, causes difficulty for women. After having been harassed, numerous Assyrian Christian women have opted to wear the Muslim hijab for security purposes.[149]

After capturing cities in Iraq, ISIL issued guidelines on how to wear clothes and veils. ISIL warned women in the city of Mosul to either wear full-face veils or face severe punishment.[150] A cleric told Reuters in Mosul that ISIL gunmen had ordered him to read out the warning in his mosque when worshippers gathered. ISIL ordered the faces of both male and female mannequins to be covered, in an order that also banned the use of naked mannequins.[151] In Ar-Raqqah, the group uses its two battalions of female fighters in the city to enforce compliance by women with its strict laws on individual conduct.[152] ISIL released 16 notes labeled "Contract of the City," a set of rules aimed at civilians in Nineveh. One rule stipulated that women should stay at home and not go outside unless necessary.[153]

---

[149] US Department of State, 2010.
[150] "Islamic State says women in Mosul must wear full veil or be punished." The Irish Times. 26 July 2014
[151] Ibid.
[152] "ISIS is actively recruiting female fighters to brutalize other women." Business Insider.
[153] Taylor Adam (12 June 2014). "The rules in ISIS' new state: Amputations for stealing and women to stay indoors." The Washington Post. August 2014.

The ongoing threats of violence forces Assyrian women to adapt to Islamic rule and, thus, seriously restricts their freedom of movement. This limitation, in turn, exacerbates the resource dilemma because access to education and employment are restricted. From 2015 to 2018, Assyrians have been subjected illegal land grabs, removal of local Assyrian officials, discrimination, and oppression. Despite the obvious adverse conditions for Assyrians in the Middle East, Assyrian leadership globally stagnates to a struggle for hegemony and notoriety.

SECTION III—THE ASSYRIAN RESOURCE DILEMMA

CHAPTER SEVEN – HEGEMONY CLASH

In the twentieth century, as a result of the international community's ignorance regarding the Assyrian struggle for independence, several collectivist organizations were cultivated by a new generation of freethinking Assyrians. These organizations were secular rather than spiritual and began documenting international law and human rights violations against the Assyrian people by utilizing and applying traditional and contemporary ideals. Those ideals included political rights for Assyrians, human rights for Assyrians, legal protection and representation, and prohibition of discriminatory practices by a government establishment. Young Assyrian university students began reading literature concerning human rights and freedom and began to develop resentment for the then-prevailing structure of authority that was based on old tribal and religious ideologies, which had been the impetus behind most of these organizations. Some of the organizations embraced egalitarian ideals, coupled with democratic principles that were averse to monarchies and dictatorships governing the Middle East. The members of the groups would anonymously pass out information to other Assyrians and oppressed minorities in the Middle East, urging them to educate themselves and dissent against authority.

One of the first Assyrian organizations to demonstrate awareness of Assyrian autonomy was the Assyrian Democratic Movement, also known as Zowaa. The Assyrian Democratic Movement demonstrates its dedication to the Assyrian cause in Iraq by satisfying Assyrian political objectives through the allocation of resources and security for the Assyrian people living in Iraq. Zowaa operates as the general source of authority in Iraq for Assyrians; currently, Yonadam Kanna, the president of Zowaa, serves as an Assyrian representative in the Iraqi Parliament.[154]

Another Assyrian political group that arose after World War II was the Assyrian Universal Alliance (AUA). Established in 1968, the Assyrian Universal Alliance was created as a worldwide organization to

---

[154] www.zowaa.org

spread, uphold, and enhance the Assyrian name around the world, to secure the human rights of the Assyrian people in their homeland, and to obtain an autonomous region in the Assyrian ancestral homeland. In 1991, the Assyrian Universal Alliance became a member of the Unrepresented Nations and Peoples Organization (UNPO).[155] And there is yet another organization: In 1957, Assyrians formed the Assyrian Democratic Organization in Syria, but it has been continuously restricted by Syrian authorities from political activity in Syria.[156]

Many Assyrian men and women began to join these organizations around the world. The Assyrian Democratic Movement and the Assyrian Universal Alliance have regional offices in countries throughout the world, including the United States, Australia, Sweden, England, France, Syria, Iran, and Iraq. Simultaneously, while pledging to these secular organizations, most Assyrians still claim allegiance and follow the teachings of religious institutions.

One religious institution is The Assyrian Church of the East, which is located in the United States, Australia, Sweden, England, Germany, Syria, Iran, Iraq, India, and China. Together, the Assyrian Church of the East and most political organizations have a cordial and favorable relationship, thus demonstrating respect for each other's causes. However, political organizations, individual politicians, and the church have incidentally conflicted with one another, which has precluded Assyrian independence by inducing an incendiary effect within the Assyrian nation. This conflict has caused the Assyrian population to partake in the politics of anger, inducing organizations with germane purposes to compete as reactionary forces. This has caused a dilemma between groups, which induces demagoguery that has increased bitterness and virulence in Assyrian politics.

---

[155] www.aua.net
[156] Assyrian International News Agency. "The Assyrian Democratic Organization rejects the Iraqi constitution." August 25, 2005. Retrieved from http://www.aina.org/news/20050904120844.htm

Social psychology has shown that people gain almost as much satisfaction from reducing the winnings of those who seem to have gotten them unfairly as from receiving a modest portion of such winnings for themselves. For years, this has been the norm as practiced by the Assyrian political organization, glorifying their political group through resentment and at the expenditure of another political organization. Historian Richard Hofstadter wrote a famous essay about the recurring strain of, as he put it, "a paranoid style in ... politics"— referring to an "underlying readiness among average individuals to see conspiracies among powerful elites supposedly plotting against them."[157]

This type of paranoia in the Assyrian community has stemmed from global economic stress, devastating conditions in the Middle East, ignorance by international communities, and inefficient Assyrian political organizations. Paranoia of prolonged stress has opened the door to demagogues rather than leaders to gain and maintain power. Assyrians now feel threatened and unhinged from their culture, indigenous land, and freedom and increasingly look to authority figures that promise simple remedies proffering scapegoats. Demagoguery brings out the worst in followers, "incites hate, scapegoats the powerless as a means of fortifying power, and exploits people's irrational fears."[158]

---

[157] Richard J. Hofstadter. Paranoid Style in American Politics" Harpers Magazine. November 1964.
[158] Robert Reich. "The Difference between a Demagogue and Leaders." October 26, 2015. Accessed March 18, 2016. http://www.newsweek.com/difference-between-leader-and-demagogue-387257.

Assyrians are susceptible to extreme conservative ideology because of self-loathing and internalized oppression[159] attributed to shock from genocide, past discrimination, and geographic displacement. Extreme conservative ideology, most notably in the Anglosphere, is focused on private morality, religion, and wealth. The 2016 United States presidential election was contentious among Assyrians. Although there is very limited data on Assyrian voting patterns in 2016, social media demonstrates that Assyrians voted and were spontaneously enthusiastic for Donald Trump, whose campaign reflects the hyperboles of the radical conservatives in the United States. Within the Anglosphere and Europe, extremists have abandoned the pretense of "normal parliamentary party" and have become a radical community.[160] Extreme conservatives' preoccupation with the corporate sector and the very wealthy have caused right wing political parties to "reach out to evangelical Christian groups, slave-holding states in the United States, nativists, and candidates use hyperboles creating a spectacle of entertainment."[161] According to conservative contributor Rod Dreher, conservatives, in America, are prepared to "wreck things to get their way." "The Republicans cannot govern … they are radicals."[162]

---

[159] According to psychologists, self-loathing refers to an extreme dislike or hatred of oneself, or being angry at or even prejudiced against oneself. The term is also used to designate a dislike or hatred of a group, family, social class, or stereotype to which one belongs and/or has. Internalized oppression refers to when people are targeted, discriminated against, or oppressed over a period of time; they often internalize (believe and make part of their self-image – their internal view of themselves) the myths and misinformation that society communicates to them about their group.
[160] Noam Chomsky. Who Rules the World? Ch. 21. Pg. 219. New York, NY: Metropolitan, 2016.
[161] Rod Dreher. "Republicans, Over the Cliff." The American Conservative. September 30, 2013. Accessed March 10, 2016.
[162] Ibid

Conservative groups have persuaded Assyrian groups to focus on religious conflicts between Arabs and Assyrians. "Religion, for many individuals or groups, may be an expression of serene belief, personal peace, and charity of mind. But for some militant spirits it may also be a source or an outlet for animosities."[163] The Assyrians disdain for Islam is prioritized and preyed upon concurrently with a focus on privacy in matters such as marriage and contraception further exacerbating religious fundamentalism within local Assyrian communities. The effect on Assyrian communities within the Anglosphere is that participation within the Assyrian community is precluded due to ideological, religious, and lifestyle differences.

When civic organizing dwindles in participation among Assyrians, political groups become homogenous in religious substance without discussing countervailing views. Then, groups tend to favor their own biases without proper checks and balances from opposing opinions impeding alternative perspectives. For example, church groups and congregants support new Republican radicalism in the United States by applying principles of the wealthy and powerful rather than indigenous rights or the traditional Assyrian Church of the East Gospels' concern over preferential treatment of the poor. Further, the focus on Christianity has usurped an indigenous perspective for Assyrian rights which inaccurately portrays the Assyrian cause as that of exclusive religious rights rather than inclusive secular organizing.

Thus, confidence in accumulating resources and tolerance for vulnerable and overlooked people is superseded by unnecessary conflicts caused by external factors of conservative radicalism. Consequently, unnecessary conflicts preclude social cohesion within local Assyrian communities, thus causing a lack of confidence in Assyrian cultural satisfaction. Also, Assyrians lack confidence in institutions unreasonably fear for their safety, causing less tolerance to help one another and other vulnerable and overlooked groups, dividing Assyrians into competing and mutually exclusive conflicting secular and religious factions.

---

163 Richard Hofstader. Anti-intellectualism in American Life. Ch. 5 Pg. 118. Vintage Books. New York 1963.

Examples of demagogues pin pointing on Assyrians would be the Prosperity Gospel Church and its media outlets, such as the Trinity Broadcasting Network (TBN) and the Christian Broadcast Network (CBN). The Prosperity Gospel is a purportedly religious doctrine that financial blessing is the will of God for Christians, and that faith, positive speech, and donations to certain Christian ministries will increase one's material wealth. TBN and CBN pontificate the exchange of money for personal empowerment, which leads to Assyrians in financial or personal distress donating to church groups that have no denomination and are directed by illegitimate authority. Further, CBN utilizes its media power to incite fear and hate in the Assyrian community. CBN published an article titled "She Fled Iran But Was Murdered Here by an 'Islamic Fanatic,'" about Benetta Bet-Badal, a victim of the terror attacks in San Bernardino in December 2015. The article fixates on the religious conflict between Muslims and Christians in the Middle East. Rather than praising Bet-Badal's culture, achievements, and support, CBN emphasized that immigrant Assyrian Americans are at equivalent risk of Islamic extremism in the United States to their former homelands by implying in the article that "Christians Not Being Safe, Even in America."[164]

Another source of demagoguery preying on Assyrians are private interest organizations that wish to exploit vulnerable groups such as the Assyrians for monetary gain through "facades of seemingly eleemosynary donations" to Assyrians. One group includes the National Rifle Association (NRA), which recently has taken an inordinate interest protecting Assyrians in the Middle East while simultaneously earning the most profitable returns for their members from the conflicts in the Middle East; an estimated $6 billion U.S.[165]

---

[164] Christian Broadcasting Network. "She Fled Iran, But Was Murdered Here by an 'Islamic Fanatic'" December 5, 2015. Accessed March 18, 2016. http://www.cbn.com/cbnnews/us/2015/December/She- Fled-Iran-But-Was Murdered-in-America-by-Islamic-Fanatic/.
[165] Vice News. 2015 19 May. Rearming Iraq: The New Arms Race in the Middle East. Retrieved from https://www.youtube.com/watch?v=tIzn45hcNLQ

The NRA's message of bearing arms is adverse to a peaceful outcome for the Assyrian community. According to UC Berkeley Professor, Richard Hassner, the most important influence on the shape of war has not come from the weapons used or the soldiers who participate in war but from societies on behalf of whom the war is taking place. Societies are an important influence on the shape of war; stakeholders cannot be separated from weapons, technology, or soldiers who participate. Soldiers, weapons, and the doctrine of the society are interrelated: one cannot examine the effects of one without examining the others. Therefore, placing guns and ammunition in a chaotic region without genuinely and sincerely examining the region will lead to more useless bloodshed.

Paranoia and demagoguery have risen to help cause a resource dilemma within the Assyrian global population. In order to preempt the demagoguery or bitterness contained in populism in the Assyrian community, secular political reform must take place before the resource dilemma gets too far out of hand.

CHAPTER EIGHT – WHAT IS THE ASSYRIAN RESOURCE DILEMMA?

A resource is defined as collective wealth, a source of supply, support, or aid, especially one that can be readily drawn upon when needed.[166] A dilemma is defined as a situation requiring a choice between equally undesirable alternatives.[167] The Assyrian resource dilemma can be defined as the impact of collective assets of Assyrians being substantially outweighed by the consequences of an undesirable choice to donate to either church or political development, thus causing resources to be scarce.

An asset includes any tangible or intangible resource worth of value. Liabilities are conveniently defined as any outlay, expenditures, or detriments facing Assyrians, whether financial or theoretical. Therefore, a resource dilemma worsens as liabilities substantially outweigh the Assyrian global community assets. Consequently, the effect of the resource dilemma has been a conflict of power that has reduced the wherewithal of assets and caused confusion regarding who is accountable for the lack of Assyrian development. Development means "escaping foreign domination," and "providing solutions to the most critical, interrelated social problems: poverty, unemployment, and inequality.[168]

In the interest of clarity, the term "resource dilemma" applies to the collective national funds to which Assyrian groups attempt to allocate supplies when needed. Resource dilemma does not refer to the capital/income/wealth ratio of individual Assyrians. Many Assyrians around the world enjoy success and wealth; thus. resource dilemma is imprecise when applied to a single Assyrian or family. Although individual Assyrians donate the lion's share of Assyrian collective funds, donation sizes and amounts vary from individual to individual.

---

[166] Dictionary.com. Define, Resource.
[167] Dictionary.com. Define, Dilemma.
[168] Richard J. Barnett & Ronald E. Müller. Global Reach: The Power of the Multinational Corporations. Simon & Schuster. New York. 1974

Therefore, it is important to examine the crux of the resource dilemma in detail, regarding closely why some individual Assyrians enjoy wealth while concurrently the Assyrian nation as one suffers from a resource dilemma. Concurrently, people's short-term selfish interests are at odds with long-term group interests and the common good; thus, a resource dilemma more often than not arises when too many group members choose to pursue individual profit and immediate satisfaction rather than behave in the group's best long-term interests.[169]

There are obvious difficulties in solving the resource dilemma within the Assyrian community; first, Assyrians are spread out in many different countries, which complicates the continuity between Assyrians in the diaspora. The political factions regarding Assyrian leadership and organizations lead to competition between groups with identical goals for donations in an already limited community. And second, numerous Assyrians around the world live in unfavorable circumstances. These difficulties pose an obvious struggle; however, it is possible to converge resources together through the international cooperation of Assyrians living in the diaspora and the regional political integration between Assyrian leadership.

Within the Assyrian population are dissenting factions between the Assyrian Church of the East and Assyrian political organizations. These factions have caused conflict, and that conflict has created controversy and controversy-induced division among the Assyrian people. Assyrian fundraising has been spread thin as the Assyrian people donate to both religious and political groups, which causes an unhelpful discrepancy in terms of financial support that is vital to the progress and growth of the Assyrian nation.

Because the Assyrian Church of the East values tradition, history, and antiquity, the church has been able to maintain its identity and spread the gospel around the world. The Assyrian Church of the East has built churches, missionaries, hospitals, shelters, and, in some

---

[169] S. T. Allison, J. K., Beggan, & E.H., Midgley, (1996). The quest for "Similar Instances" and "Simultaneous Possibilities:" Metaphors in social dilemma research. Journal of Personality and Social Psychology, 71, pp 479-497.

cases, educational institutions for the Assyrian people in Iraq, Iran, and Syria.

Political organizations such as Zowaa build schools and, homes, provide security, distribute warm clothing for cold winters, food, and shelter to disadvantaged Assyrian families in the Middle East. Additionally, the Assyrian Universal Alliance has been actively pursuing Assyrian interests in the international community through the United Nations, the UN Human Rights Council, and the United Nations' Declaration of Minority Rights.

Both the Church of the East and these political organizations are committed to maintaining Assyrian identity. However, the conflict of financial support has caused Assyrian progression to be spread thin by the polarization of beliefs between various groups of Assyrians regarding the means of progression. Many supporters of Zowaa and the AUA have turned distrusting of church because of the political conflict with the Church of the East.[170] As a result, Assyrians who were once members of these two political organizations have resigned their positions and exclusively support the Assyrian Church of the East. This type of division of political monetary support creates the hazard of scarce resources.

Moreover, scarce resources are caused by peculiar and redundant appropriations by both the Assyrian Church of the East and political organizations. The Assyrian Church of the East continues to build churches in Iraq and Iran for Assyrian Christians. The Assyrian Church of the East's attempt to maintain its Christian foundation in Iraq has proven to be ineffective. The financial resources to support a church in Iraq are not productive because the Assyrian population is dwindling in the Middle East, and there are already a large number of churches in which Assyrians can congregate.

---

[170] According to Wikileaks Cable: 09BAGHDAD1785_a, Kanna was dismissive of the influence of the religious leaders saying that the "people viewed them as corrupt and out of touch."

Political organizations have furthered the resource dilemma toward their own funds as well. These organizations have been operating for over decades and have not protected and maintained Assyrian identity in an effective manner because of the lack of support and signals of inefficient fundraising from mishandling 501 (c)(3) nonprofit laws in America.

Nonprofit 501(c)(3) groups in America are confirmed by the Internal Revenue Service (IRS) and are exempt from federal income tax if activities are charitable, religious, educational, or foster amateur sports.[171] According to Small Business Taxes and Management Group, an approved 501(c)(3) exemption allows donors to the organization to reduce their own taxable incomes by deducting the amounts of their donations given and, thus, to reduce their personal income taxes. Further, the IRS permits 501(c)(3) organizations to avoid federal income taxes on the difference between revenues (donations, grants, service fees) received versus expenses (wages, supplies, state and local taxes paid, etc.) from its main operations. Zowaa and the AUA are supported and rely on affiliate Assyrian organizations such as the Assyrian American National Federation (AANF) and Assyrian Aid Society (AAS). Both AANF and AAS are 501(c)(3) and support Zowaa and the Assyrian Universal Alliance by throwing annual Assyrian conventions and art galas to help unite Assyrians in a diaspora and raise funds for Assyrian progression. However, 501(c)(3) fundraising is dubious because charitable groups are not required to be transparent to their donors or beneficiaries except for an annual report to the IRS. The lack of transparency leads to private benefits and inurnment to the group's members, which distorts and misrepresents actual Assyrian progression. Further, 501(c)(3) laws limit the political influence these organizations have on American policymakers because expenditures on lobbying and political activities are restricted to 5 percent of the group's revenue, therefore limiting the amount of resources that can be accumulated from non-Assyrian lobbying and political activity.

---

[171] How to lose your 501(c)(3) tax-exempt status (without ... (n.d.). Retrieved March 21, 2016, from https://www.irs.gov/PUP/charities/charitable/How to Lose Your Tax Exempt Status.pdf

Although, both the AANF and the AAS have been operating for over 25 years as tax- exempt organizations, neither has been successful in accumulating funds for large expenditures for Assyrian development. Both the AANF and the AAS are not democratic and transparent in their fundraising techniques, which has caused ineffective dark fundraising contributing to the Assyrian resource dilemma.

Furthermore, Assyrian 501(c)(3) organizations lack proper leadership in key developed countries such as the United States, England, Australia, and Sweden. The lack of leadership within these political organizations is causing firstly, a lack of transparency in accounting practices, secondly, poor communication between these political organizations and the Assyrian people they are attempting to serve, and lastly irresponsibly scapegoating each organization's responsibility to the Assyrian people. Additionally, the leadership in these organizations does not have the expertise to allocate resources for a nation in a diaspora. They are strangers, moreover, to the burdens and problems of operational responsibility and the unceasing pressure for immediate decisions.[172] The number of Assyrians joining political organizations is dwindling, which leads these organizations to focus on marketing for the justification of the status quo and increasing membership rather than fulfilling their goals.

The Assyrian nation's inexact disposition on leadership and accountability has precluded Assyrian progression. The Assyrian nation does not have a uniform organization that is accountable for Assyrian progression. The lack of uniformity causes resources to be spread among countries, cities, churches, and organizations. There are an estimated 40 Assyrian political groups around the world, and none have any monetary connection with one another.

---

[172] Saul Alinksy. Rules for Radicals. Random House. 1979. P. 25

This type of separation of capital is an example of Assyrians precluding their own progression. An ideal solution to this problem would be to consolidate the organization's resources based on their goals or agenda. However, this has not been pragmatically applied historically because new Assyrian organizations are cultivated in response to a falling out from an original Assyrian organization, thus spreading resources to redundant organizations that are for the same cause but hinder each other's progression. The Assyrian nation's resource problem is the key paradigm of the Assyrian struggle for independence. In order to overcome this resource dilemma, Assyrians must accomplish a national bargain intended for regional political integration and international cooperation, to learn how to allocate resources efficiently by every politically active Assyrian, regardless of association. Therefore, to help overcome this resource dilemma, there must be a national bargain among all Assyrians to learn how to modify the process of accumulating finances, organization, unity, and solidarity.

In order to overcome the resource dilemma, Assyrian associations must learn to organize and allocate resources adequately, with the maximum combinations of goods and services, efficiently using available resources and technology within a given period of time. To organize means "figuring out how to manage large research projects that are exposed to high levels of volatility, dividing tasks into components undertaken by different groups, with pieces that can be put together."[173]

---

[173] Joseph Stiglitz. Creating a Learning Society. Pg.49-50. Columbia University Press. New York. 2014

Assyrian organizations must continue to expand their learning capabilities with education and anticipate "lifelong learning," enhancing the ability to adapt to an ever-changing world.[174] Access to knowledge is vital to expand capabilities because all knowledge builds on preexisting knowledge.[175] A "culture of openness ensuring access to knowledge can be the catalysts for learning because one idea can incite new ideas-even if the new idea does not use the old idea or build on it directly."[176] The cultural catalysts will help construct a "creative mindset conducive to learning, that entails the belief that change is possible and important-and can be shaped and advanced by deliberate activities."[177] In other words, "we believe what we believe partly because those that we talk to believe similarly."[178] When Assyrians interact on the foundation that developmental change is possible then the beliefs will confront reality, which provides an impetus of change in beliefs. Establishing capacity for contacts beyond Assyrian culture is important because interactions can catalyze learning. Learning from other people can, "provide the knowledge input that is the basis of learning and provide the catalyst which enhances innovation."[179] Also, "universities, and research institutions enhance the range and depth of contacts. Structured interaction can be better-that is, organizational architectures can help bring individuals who might stimulate each other into contact."[180]

---

[174] Ibid. Pg. 57-58.
[175] Ibid. P. 58
[176] Ibid. P.59
[177] Ibid. Pg. 61-62
[178] Ibid. P. 71
[179] Ibid. P. 60
[180] Ibid. Pg.60-61

SECTION IV—THE ASSYRIAN COMPROMISE

CHAPTER NINE – THE ASSYRIAN INTERNATIONAL COMPROMISE

The twenty-first century has changed through a transformation of politics and economics from policies implemented in the twentieth century. "National economies no longer exist."[181] Private wealth significantly outnumbers public national wealth. "All that remains rooted within national borders are the people who comprise a nation."[182] Each nation's primary asset is its citizen's skills and insights. "As borders become ever more meaningless in economic terms, those citizens best positioned to thrive in the world market are tempted to slip the bonds of national allegiance and, by so doing, disengage themselves from their favored fellows."[183]

Assyrians in the diaspora are living within this transformation to a new form of mercantilism, which surmises that "nation-states are seeking to produce and advance at the expense of another nation-state while national wealth pertains only to a sovereign, rather than to the well-being of ordinary individuals within the nation."[184] Thus, it is vitally imperative that each Assyrian acknowledges another as members of the same nation despite not inhabiting the same economy because acknowledgment of unity determines how strong the nation's loyalty remains toward the goal of Assyrian development. Loyalty to the nation would correspond with economic self- interest, thus inducing individual citizens to support education and other civic improvements, even when the individual was likely to enjoy but a fraction of what was sacrificed in the short term because it was assumed that such sacrifices would be amply rewarded eventually.

However, in the twentieth and twenty-first century, Assyrian organizations did not adopt this type of logic to the accumulation of resources. Rather, political organizations rallied against other Assyrian organizations and politicians by exalting their own achievements at the

---

[181] Robert Reich. The Work of Nations. Vintage Books. New York. 1991
[182] Ibid.
[183] Robert Reich. The Work of Nations. Vintage Books. P.136 New York. 1991
[184] Ibid.

expense of other Assyrians. Organizations claim their "rails are necessary to confirm their patriotism"[185] and reassure Assyrian donors that their resources are being effectively utilized. However, this manufactured praise only gives rise to self-righteousness about their own supposed accomplishments relative to the totality of circumstances of Assyrians to attempt to obtain a publicly favorable reputation. These justifications are misleading because they suggest that the desired know-how to solve the Assyrian resource dilemma is somehow absorbed by these organizations only. This is not the case because other entities such as churches, nonprofits, and foreign aid can contribute to Assyrian progression in proportion to Assyrian political organizations.

The fact that the strength of the Assyrian population is synonymous with the proximity, profitability, and productivity of current Assyrian political organizations is an axiom on the brink of furthering the resource dilemma to disorder. The strength of the Assyrian population is not rooted within current Assyrian political organizations nor those political organizations with proximity to the Middle East, but to any group which includes any type of individual Assyrian and learns how to "accumulate resources and disseminate the resources" to add more value to the Assyrian community, therefore "increasing their own worth."[186] As Assyrians attempt to grow wealthier and more productive in Western societies, their ability to produce for Assyrian progression has only reached individual status and falls short to benefit Assyrian progression as a whole.

Therefore, the Assyrians' political leadership must spread democratic ideas genuinely and sincerely to induce others to utilize their skills acquired in Western societies in order to increase the power of their organizations and improve the well-being of the Assyrian nation as a whole and not just exalt individuals that support a particular political organization or pecuniary interest.

Political philosopher Edmund Burke contended that a nation constituted a contract, a form of "partnership not only between those

---

[185] Work of Nations. P. 137
[186] Work of Nations. P. 137

who are living but between those who are to be born."[187] "The partnership was a moral one; citizens had obligations to one another. Democratic institutions provided a means of both instilling and fulfilling such obligations simultaneously."[188] John Stuart Mill, the English philosopher, argued that democracy cultivated moral attachments "by the utmost possible publicity and discussion, whereby not merely a few individuals in succession, but the whole public, are made, to a certain extent, participants in the government."[189] Therefore, these scholars argue that democratic institutions created good citizens.

In turn, good citizens are diligent, socially responsive, and willing to sacrifice their lives and property for their nation. A good citizen may transform easily into a patriot. The English philosopher Bolingbroke expressed the spirit of patriotism, in which it is observed that every citizen who was a real patriot would "direct all his thoughts and actions to the good of his country"—that is, "to the good of the people."[190] As the idea of the nation grew, so did the idea that people owed a greater allegiance to all humanity. "Thomas Jefferson and Benjamin Franklin regarded themselves as citizens of the world, as did Goethe, Schiller, and Kant in Germany; Voltaire, Diderot, and Helvetius in France; and Goldsmith and Hume in Britain. Their focus was on the universal rights and duties of man."[191]

These political philosophers induced many cultures to become aware of their national identities. Thus, the populations of Central and Eastern Europe had already become interested in their native cultures, partly in reaction to the political domination of Austrians and Turks and the cultural domination of the French. In 1784, J. G. von Herder, a protestant theologian, had "called upon Germans to stop emulating the French and develop their own national character"—their common

---

[187] Edmund Burke, Reflections on the Revolution in France. Penguin. New York 1968, Vol. 2
[188] Ibid. P. 321
[189] John Stuart Mill, "Representative Government" in Utilitarianism, On Liberty and Representative Government. Everyman's Library. London. 1910.
[190] Bolingbroke's Works. (London: T. Davies, ed., 1775) Vol. 1.
[191] Work of Nations. P. 16

German spirit, or Volksgeist, meaning "spirit" or "character" in German. Herder continues to explain that other "national groups had their own Volksgeist as well, which they should seek to uncover."[192], [193]Joseph Mazzini, moral philosopher and politician, told Italians that "their duty to the nation was intermediate between their duty to family and to God." "National consciousness spread throughout Europe during subsequent decades: Poles, Magyars, Russians, Czechs, Slovaks, Ruthenians, Romanians, Serbs, Croatians, and Greeks all became self-consciously national, even if they lacked their own nation state."[194]

Drawing analogies to eighteenth-century Europe, Assyrian organizations must abide by democratic and transparent institutions to help spread national consciousness throughout the Assyrian global community. The potential rise of reasonable nationalistic patriotism may contribute to progress and develop effective momentum toward a strong identity, which, in turn, may lead to a surge of democratic principles transforming into a recognized nation-state. Furthermore, democratic administration depends on committed and educated populations, and their common defense will be proved better with citizen patriots than fighters based on recruitment. The idea of Assyria and economic nationalism can be accomplished, however, despite Assyrians today living in a far more different world than Europeans in the eighteenth century. Therefore, it is important to discuss the Assyrians' current and future global predicament, which, unfortunately, yields dimidiating power.

---

[192] Ibid.
[193] J.G. Herder. Ideas on the Philosophy of the History of Mankind. 1784
[194] Work of Nations. P. 18

CHAPTER TEN – DIMINUTIVE POPULATION, PECUINARY INTEREST, AND GLOBALIZATION

The world population is the total number of living humans on Earth; as of today, it is estimated to be 7.096 billion, according to the United States Census Bureau (USCB). These 7 billion people "take 93,000 commercial flights a day from 9000 airports[195], drive 1 billion cars[196], and carry 7 billion mobile phones around with them"—the phones can "monitor heart rates, purchase stocks, post restaurant reviews, share family photos, tweet real-time information about unfolding events."[197] The Assyrian population is estimated to be around 1 to 2 million globally. That places the Assyrian nation at less than .1 percent of the current global population. This is critical, because the Assyrians are in a diaspora around the world in which, economic and social circumstances vary substantially from individual to individual and family to family, depending on a wide variety of factors. Such factors include income, economic conditions, inequality, and globalization.

---

[195] "All Scheduled Flights Worldwide," http: www.flixxy.com/scheduled-airline-flights-worldwide.htm.

[196] Daniel Tencer, "The Number of Cars Worldwide Surpasses 1 Billion; Can The World Handle This. Many Wheels?" The Huffington Post Canada, February 19, 2013, http://www.huffingtonpost.ca/2011/08/23/car-population_n_934291.html.

[197] Joshua Pramis, "Number of Mobile Phones to exceed world population by 2014" Digital Trends, February 18, 2013, http:/ /www.digitaltrends.com/mobile/mobile-phone-world-population-2014/.

National income is defined as "the sum of all income available to the residents of a given country in a given year, regardless of the legal classification of that income."[198] "The classifications of income are labor income from wages, salary, honoraria, bonuses, and capital income from profits, dividends, interest, rents, royalties." "Income is a flow. It corresponds to the quantity of goods produced and distributed in a given period (which we generally take to be a year). Capital is a stock. It corresponds to the total wealth owned at a given point in time."[199] This stock comes from the wealth appropriated or accumulated in all prior years combined. "The most natural way to measure the capital stock in a particular country is to divide that stock by annual flow of income. That is the capital/income ratio."[200]

In developed countries where Assyrians reside today, the capital/income ratio generally varies between "5 and 6 years and the capital consists almost entirely of private capital."[201] Some Assyrians are wealthy, some live-in poverty, some are wealthy in poor countries, some are poor in wealthy countries, but most retain around the average median income of their respective domiciles. For example, Assyrians in America live in a service base and consumption economy, which may be beneficial or burdening for Assyrians depending on their wealth and power. In the United States, Britain, France, and Germany, the national income was roughly $31,000-$36,000 per capita in 2010 whereas total private wealth was typically on the order of $151,000-$201,000, which is five to six times annual national income.[202]

---

[198] Thomas Piketty. Capital in the Twenty-First Century. Pg. 43
[199] Ibid.
[200] Ibid.
[201] Thomas Piketty. Capital in the Twenty-First Century. Pg. 50
[202] Ibid.

In regards to Assyrians and global income inequality, it is essential to divide the Assyrian population by 3 segments of the world within the scope of the Assyrian diaspora. Then estimate and analyze social mobility through available data of the respective segments in which Assyrians reside. One segment involves the Anglosphere countries, such as Australia, Canada, Great Britain, and United States. Another segment consists Sweden, Germany, France, Denmark, and other European countries. The last segment includes Middle Eastern countries.

Middle Eastern Countries

In the Middle East, the focus of economic inequality derives from petroleum rents, privilege, and power from royal families, theocracy, or dictatorships supported by foreign governments. Because data on inequality are limited in the Middle East due to unreliable fiscal sources, inequality for Assyrians in Middle Eastern countries is presented differently from those of other segments. The data provided for Middle Eastern Assyrians are based on "regional inequality in the aggregate from distribution of population and average income from Middle East using national accounts and a plausible hypothesis."[203] The tentative conclusions reached were that the Middle East taken as a whole is "highly unequal by international and historical standards."[204]

---

[203] Facundo Alvaredo, Thomas Piketty. Measuring top incomes and inequality in the Middle East. Economic Research Forum. Giza, Egypt. pg. 10
[204] Ibid.

The population in the Middle East is estimated to be 294.1 million.[205] Within the region, an estimated 200,000 Assyrians reside in Iraq, 70,000 in Iran, 150,000 in Syria, 150,000 in Jordan, 40,000 in Lebanon, 2,500 in the United Arab Emirates, and 1,000 in Kuwait. Iran makes up 26 percent of the region's population with 18 percent share of the Middle East national income.[206] Iraq, Syria, Jordan, and Lebanon combined make up close to 30 percent of the Middle East population and earn 11.8 percent of national income from the region. Oil countries make up 16 percent and hold 59 percent of the region's national income, with the UAE and Kuwait holding 12 percent of the population but accumulating over 21 percent of national income in the region.[207]

Thus, inequality in the Middle East is higher compared with that of the United States, Europe, and emerging and developing countries in Latin America and East Asia. The reasoning for high inequality in the Middle East varies.

One reason for this inequality may be due to pathological influence from foreign governments, which has caused dysfunction through decades of dictatorships repressing the general population. Further, that same foreign influence induces Middle Eastern countries to rely on the continuous consumption of petroleum rents. Thus, royal powers' main focus is claims to status, privilege, and power focused on inheritance to solidify dynastic wealth rather than social mobility for the general populations.

---

[205] Ibid.
[206] Ibid.
[207] Ibid.

Another view is neo-liberalism, which was illustrated earlier through details of the United States' invasion of Iraq, which involves foreign influence that drains a country's resources for privatized profit. For example, according to Wikileaks, Al-Sabah published a report citing Yonadum Kanna, a member of the Economic and Construction Committee in the outgoing parliament, as saying, "the next parliament will continue implementing the projects of privatizing a number of public establishments with the aim of achieving economic progress."[208]

Regardless of which of these views one adopts, the reality for Middle Eastern Assyrians is that Assyrians lack consistent social and economic participation in daily life.[209] For example, an Assyrian stated about Northern Iraq, that "systemic discrimination prohibits them from integrating into the community." Another Assyrian internist, who fled to the Kurdish Regional Government (KRG) in February 2008, said, "He receives only $300 per month for his work at a KRG health clinic and is not compensated based on his experience and expertise." Kurdish doctors with similar skills are paid much more, he said, and claimed discrepancies in pay between Kurds and Assyrian IDPs can be found in several fields. Those who do work have found security and limited financial support from the KRG, yet still face systematic discrimination and economic woes. Further, access to resources is difficult for Assyrians. According to Wikileaks, Father Warda, a priest living in Iraq, noted, "poor infrastructure, lack of roads, schools, health clinics, and agricultural equipment." Gave precluded "even basic community planning that would help and could be used to solicit funds from European donors."[210]

Anglosphere countries

Anglosphere countries are English-speaking with a population of 449.1 million that have seen a rise in economic inequality since the 1980s. The share of top percentiles in total income rose since the 1970s

---

[208] Al-Sahab. Iraq-Iraq-Middle-East. Wikileaks cable: GI files 821824.
[209] OECD (2016), Society at a glance 2016: OECD social indicators, OECD Publishing, Paris.
   DOI: http://dx.doi.org/10.1787/9789264261488-en
[210] Iraqi Embassy. RRT Erbil: NEA-I Director discusses minority rights during KRG visit. Wikileaks cable: 08BAGHDAD1830_a. June 28 2008

in all Anglosphere countries but with different magnitudes. During the 1970's, the "upper centile's share of national income was quite similar"[211] across the Anglosphere. In the United States with unofficial estimates of 400,000 Assyrians residing in America, the top 1 percent share of national income is over 20 percent.[212] In Britain, unofficial estimates of 15,000-20,000 Assyrians reside in there while the top 1 percent share of national income is 15 percent.[213] In Canada, the population of Assyrians is estimated around 40,000 with the 1 percent sharing 14 percent of national income.[214] While Australia has an estimated 45,000 Assyrians, the top 1 percent shares 10 percent of national income.[215]

The Anglosphere countries' economic inequality of income has accelerated substantially since the 1980s. For example, a recent demonstration by research depicted income inequality soaring because the "very affluent" top 1 percent, including the 0.1, 0.01, and 0.001, in the United States have received staggering pay increases while middle class wages and income are stagnating.[216] One reason for this is due to "the explosion of very high salaries which occurred in some developed countries but not others, which suggest that policy choices caused institutional differences between the countries and not general universal causes such as globalization and technology."[217]

The rise of "supermanagers" is one reason policy choices have caused inequality. Supermanagers is a term used to describe a "group of college graduates from Anglosphere countries who pursued their studies at elite universities." Supermanagers include the "chief executive officers of Fortune 500 companies, hedge fund managers, financiers of speculation such as oil, art, commodities, coal, real estate, gold, silver." "Supermanagers" in particular have shown that "over

---

[211] Thomas Piketty. Capital in the twenty-first century. Pg. 316
[212] Thomas Piketty. Capital in the twenty-first century. Table 9.2. pg. 316
[213] Ibid. Table 9.2. pg. 316
[214] Ibid. Table 9.2. pg. 316
[215] Ibid. Table 9.2. pg. 316
[216] David, Leonhardt. Our Broken Economy, in One Simple Chart. 7 Aug. 2017, www.nytimes.com/interactive/2017/08/07/opinion/leonhardt-income-inequality.html. Accessed 9 Aug. 2017.
[217] Thomas Piketty. Capital in the twenty-first century. pg. 315

performance of the top centile explains most of the increase in the top 10 percent share of national income in English speaking countries because of the rise in income within the top 10 percent of national income earners."

"Supermanagers set their own pay based on their manipulation of the individual marginal productivity theory by stating that their job functions are unique or nearly so, that the definition of marginal productivity has regressed into a social construct for supermanagers."[218] What the rise of supermanagers means in income is that "0.1 percent of the population gets 2 to 10 percent of national income, 20 to 100 times more income than average individuals which permits elitists to occupy an influential role in social policies."[219] Within Anglosphere countries, the number of Assyrian supermanagers is unknown; however, if supermanagers are rare to any population, then the amount of Assyrian supermanagers is not likely to be high.

Assyrians immigrated in large numbers to Anglosphere countries in the late 1970s, when the structure of Anglosphere economies changed to "a sharp increase of the role of finance in the economy and a corresponding decline in domestic production."[220] Thus, Assyrians settled at a precarious time where wages flattened for workers, jobs moved abroad, technology changed, labor unions weakened, monetary speculation rose, complex financial instruments developed, and money manipulators gained ascendancy.

Anglosphere economic policy change in the late 1970s devalued Assyrian workers. Assyrians participated in societies that began "working more hours, supplementing income with multiple occupations, forgoing retirement plans, inducing borrowing thus causing consumer debt by refinancing home loans, health care debt, and student loans."[221] Anglosphere countries, notably the United States, "bought fewer consumer goods, downsized companies,

---

[218] Thomas Piketty. Capital in the twenty-first century. pg. 331-332
[219] Ibid.
[220] Noam Chomsky. Requiem for the American dream. Seven Stories Press. New York. pg. 37
[221] Jacob Kornbluth. Inequality for all. DVD

decreased tax revenue, cut government programs, educated people fewer, and unemployment was allowed to rise."[222] Therefore, for Assyrians within Anglosphere countries, particularly the United States, political direction focused on "supply-side tax cuts for wealthy political donors, deregulation of financial markets, hair-on-fire deficit reduction,[223] which causes low growth and distracts policymakers from individual economic hardships."

Assyrians in Anglosphere countries have experienced the burdens of capitalism caused by a vicious cycle of low growth. Some burdens include "less freedom, less time for leisure, less time for thought, more following order."[224] However, the primary burden for Assyrians living within the "vicious cycle"[225] in Anglosphere countries is that Assyrian resource development is hindered because inequality at the individual level is high. There is inequality separating both income from labor, and income from capital.[226] High levels of income inequality "increase political pressures, discouraging trade, investments, and hiring." Income inequality can lead affluent households to "increase savings and decrease consumption, while those with less means increase consumer borrowing to sustain consumption, and once those options run out, imbalances cannot be sustained and boom or bust cycles develop that distort the economy." These income imbalances "dampen social mobility and produce a less educated workforce that can't compete in a changing global economy." This diminishes future income prospects and potential long-term growth, thus becoming entrenched as political repercussions extend the problems.

Assyrians in proportion to regional population are not obtaining a large share of national income in any region, thus leading to high individual inequality for Assyrians, which creates a lack of

---

[222] Ibid.
[223] Dean Baker & Jared Bernstein. (2013). Getting back to full employment: A better bargain for working people. Washington, D.C.: Center for Economic and Policy Research.
[224] Noam Chomsky. Requiem for the American dream. Seven Stories Press. New York. pg. 41
[225] Jacob Kornbluth. Inequality for all. DVD
[226] Thomas Piketty. Capital in the twenty-first century. pg. 238

resources committed to alleviate the problem of the resource dilemma for all Assyrians. If Assyrians cannot maintain adequate living standards in Anglosphere countries then accumulating resources for Assyrian development will not be prioritized accordingly to accommodate the circumstances in the twenty-first century. If income concentration hinders Assyrian resource development, then it will also reduce political power and high levels of income yield. Thus, Assyrians lack power to organize and politicize to impose pressure on policymakers to recognize Assyrian struggles. And, the lack of power induces Assyrians to become passively obedient and depoliticized.

Europe

As compared with the Anglosphere, the share of the top percentile within Europe barely increased since the 1970s. Continental European countries, including the United Kingdom, have a population of 507.4 million. France makes up 13 percent of Europe's population with 15,000 Assyrians; since the 1970s, the share of national income to the top 10 percent has changed from 9 to 10 percent.[227] In Germany, 16 percent of Europe's population and 15,000 Assyrians demonstrates that the share of national income regarding the top 10 percent is 11 percent today from 9 percent in 1970s. In Sweden, where 100,000 Assyrians reside and make up 1.9 percent of Sweden's population, the top 10 percent share of national income went from 4 percent in the 1970s to 7 percent presently. Denmark, which makes up 1.1 percent of Europe's population and has 10,000 Assyrians domiciled, has seen inequality increased minutely from 5 percent in the 1980s to 7 percent now.[228]

Despite inequality rising in Sweden and Denmark, the veracity of concentration isn't extreme as in the Anglosphere, continental Europe, and the Middle East. Scandinavian countries utilized a more egalitarian economic model, which benefits Assyrians. For example, out of the entire adult population, the 10 percent receiving the highest

---

[227] Your key to European statistics. Retrieved from http://ec.europa.eu/eurostat/ the number of persons having their usual residence in a country on 1 January of the respective year. When usually resident population is not available, countries may report legal or registered residents. August 11, 2016.
[228] Ibid.

total incomes from labor and capital claim receives as little as 25 percent of total income from labor, the least well-paid 50 percent receive 30 percent of the total income, and the 40 percent in the middle receive roughly 45 percent of the total.[229] The inequality in Scandinavia is not as extreme when compared with that of the Anglospehre countries. Further, since Scandinavian countries implement adequate public funding and assistance to individuals for education, health care, and housing, the impact of high consumer debt is controlled in Sweden in a manner it is not in the Anglosphere.

In Sweden, relative to other countries, economic growth is high; Assyrian Swedes enjoy a high quality of life as a result of the robust economy. Unemployment is declining, while labor, capital, and productivity have contributed to growth, and intergenerational social mobility is high despite income concentration. Therefore, a majority of Assyrians living in Sweden have a better opportunity and higher ability to alleviate the resource dilemma. Despite the lack of data regarding Assyrians and income inequality in the diaspora, Assyrians can induce social changes from Scandinavian countries through local action that is coordinated between various Assyrians with common interests that are adequate for Assyrians demanding social progress.

Germany, France, and continental Europe share the total income of a population that is equivalent to the top 10 percent claiming 35 percent of total income, the middle 40 percent claiming 40 percent of total income, and the bottom 50 percent claiming 25 percent of total income.[230] In continental Europe, there are public programs, but these are not as egalitarian as Scandinavia. Further, inequality in continental Europe is driven by external forces such as the European Union, trade imbalances, austerity, and lack of demand in the private sector. Germany enjoys a trade and government budget surplus, while France muddles with an anemic recovery from the 2008 global great recession.

In Eastern Europe, where Assyrians reside in the Ukraine and Russia (where the population of Assyrians is estimated at 20,000), the

---

[229] Thomas Piketty. Capital in the twenty-first century. Table 7.1. pg. 247
[230] Thomas Piketty. Capital in the twenty-first century. Table 7.1. Pg. 24

population is estimated to be 200 million, and inequality is high.

Despite the lack of data on national income, indicators in the Credit-Suisse report conclude that the disparity of inequality of total income is astounding. In 2014, the share of total wealth in Russia for the top 10 percent was 84.8 percent[231], which leaves the middle 40 percent and bottom 50 percent with a spilt of 15 percent of total wealth. In Russia, the per capita monthly income is close to $1,241 a month, compared with other countries that Assyrians reside in such as Canada and the United States; $3,150 indicates that the level of inequality is just as bad if not worse than Middle Eastern countries where Assyrians are domiciled.

Assyrian groups spread out around the world benefit the least from economic inequality because income and wealth are disproportionately segregated between communities; thus, diaspora communities are negatively affected by segregation, which hinders social mobility. The Assyrian population in proportion to their respective countries averages around .3 to .7 percent of the population. Therefore, Assyrians are a small community within societies with disparities of wealth and income, which continue to diverge. Economic inequality distorts communities' continuity regarding social improvements and destabilizes Assyrians ability to fundraise collectively.

---

[231] Markus Stierle, Global Wealth Report. Credit-Suisse AG. Zurich Switzerland. 2014

All in all, besides low inequality in Scandinavia and medium inequality in some European countries, Assyrians reside in parts of the world where poverty and subsistence are realities for many. Although social mobility can be expeditiously accomplished in the Anglosphere and European countries, there are living costs that contribute to the lack of resources while pursuing professional goals and ambitions such as rent, car payments, credit card debt, student debt, healthcare debt, and low wages. While the rise of dictators, petroleum rents, and outside forces deplete the Middle East, the burdens of Assyrians within the Anglosphere trouble consumers with debt and stagnating wages, and unprecedented levels of inequality caused by oligarchy in Russia and Eastern Europe; thus, Assyrians are in a position where cooperation and integration of local secular political groups to accumulate resources for all Assyrians is imperative. If not, then the fate of Assyrians will rely on the decision of policymakers that overlook vulnerable Assyrians because officials are likely influenced by elites within the established private institutions, where decisions are discussed and prepared by agents unfamiliar with Assyrians in "executive suites and law offices within shouting distance of each other in fifteen city blocks in five major cities."[232]

Piketty, Stiglitz, and Inequality

Political economist Thomas Piketty expresses that capitalism "reinforces global inequality because the return on capital is higher than the economic growth rate of production" ($r>g$) (r symbolizes the return of private capital while g symbolizes the public growth). Capital is anything that can be "owned and generate income such as homes, stocks, and capital gains. Piketty assembled a wealth of data reinforcing increasing inequality since 1980."[233] Through this data, Piketty argues that, since 1980, capital has been growing faster than any public economy at large, and, since rich people own the capital, inequality rises, and this trend will continue.

---

[232] Noam Chomsky - Government in the future 1970. (2012, August 26). Retrieved from https://youtu.be/SnfioOtrBro
[233] Joseph Stiglitz. The Great Divide. Pg. 79

Noble Laureate Joseph Stiglitz of Columbia University stresses "r>g is not quite the right explanation, or at least not the full explanation, for the runaway growth in wealth and income inequality at the top that Piketty so thoroughly documents." Rather, Stiglitz stresses the disparity of inequality between income, and capital deriving from rents that generates wealth. Income can derive from labor or rents and is usually measured as a yearly flow of earnings.[234]

Economists refer to income derived from land as rents; it is income based not on hard work but simply on the ownership of a fixed asset.[235] Larger rents will give rise to a higher price, but a higher price for that asset would not elicit a greater supply.[236] But economists now apply the term "rents" more generally to returns other than land rents.[237] Therefore, if rents increase, there will be corresponding capital gains. Concluding that much of the increase in inequality in incomes and wealth is associated with an increase in rents and capital gains. Wealth is one's ability to accumulate a diverse portfolio of unspent rents and income. Wealth also generates its own income: interest and dividends from savings and investments.[238] It is possible that wealth could be increasing even as capital is decreasing. Therefore, an increase in wealth is possible without increasing productivity generally.

Stiglitz explains that the increase in inequality is attributable to the increase in the value of fixed assets and not the reflection of an increase in productive value. The most obvious and widespread example of wealth increasing relative to productivity is the massive rise in real estate values. If the worth of real estate increases "only to the rising price of the property it sits upon and not to physical improvements, this does not lead to a more productive economy; no workers have been hired, no wages paid, no investments made."[239] In economic terms, this gain is simply a "land rent."

---

[234] Robert Reich. Saving Capitalism for the Many not the Few. P. 92
[235] Thomas Piketty. Capital in the Twenty-First Century. P.81
[236] Ibid. pg. 81-82
[237] Ibid.
[238] Robert Reich. Saving Capitalism for the Many not the Few. P.92
[239] Thomas Piketty. Capital in the Twenty-First Century. P. 13

Some of this increase in the property value is a natural consequence of urbanization, but much is due to the financialization of the economy.[240] Financialization is the "growth of the financial sector and its increased power over the real economy including the ways the values and practices of the financial sector have shaped the rest of society."[241] An example of financialization is the increased supply of credit—credit that typically goes to those who already have wealth. "Land rents are the most obvious source of rents in the economy, but economists have identified many others, including drug pricing, copyrights, and other forms of intellectual property."[241]

The capitalized value of rents gives rise to wealth, and so if rents increase, so will wealth. If monopoly power increases, monopoly profits will increase, and so, too, will the value of the monopolies—the measured wealth of the economy. But the productivity of the economy will decrease and so, too, will the value of wages adjusted for inflation, thereby decreasing the average median income.

---

[240] Ibid.
[241] Ibid.

Furthermore, inequalities with respect to capital have been extreme in Western countries such as the United States, Canada, Great Britain, and France. The most striking fact is that, without a doubt, in all these societies, half of the population owns virtually nothing. The poorest 50 percent invariably owns less than 10 percent of the national wealth and generally less than 5 percent.[242] In particular, in the United States, the Federal Reserve (2016) indicates that the top 10 percent own 77 percent of America's wealth, while the bottom half claims just 2 percent. For the bottom half of the population, which comprises the majority of Assyrians, the very notions of wealth and capital, are relatively abstract. For millions of people, wealth amounts to little more than a few weeks' wages in a checking account or low-interest savings account, a car, and a few pieces of furniture. The inescapable reality is this: wealth is so concentrated that a large segment of the Assyrian population is virtually unaware of its existence, thus helping contribute to the resource dilemma.

Assyrians who are wealthy are minimal in number and develop a sense of power, status, and privilege because of their wealth, consequently forming a patriarchal community. This leads individuals in the community to become apathetic, divisive, or overly involved in the management of duties. Thus, those who demonstrate the latter behavior usually develop ego and narcissism that supersede the original objective intended. Also, the wealthy characteristically develop a heuristic technique approach to problem solving, learning, or discovery that employs a practical methodology not guaranteed to be optimal or perfect but that is sufficient for the immediate goals.[243]

---

[242] Matt Bruenig. Wealth Inequality Is Higher Than Ever. Retrieved from https://www.jacobinmag.com/2017/10/wealth-inequality-united-states-federal-reserve. October 1, 2017

[243] Pearl Judea. Heuristics: Intelligent Search Strategies for Computer Problem Solving. New York, Addison-Wesley, P. vii. 1983

Where finding an "optimal solution is impossible or impractical, heuristic methods can be used to speed up the process of finding a satisfactory solution."[244] Heuristics occasionally are "mental shortcuts that ease the cognitive load of making a decision."[245] Examples of this method include using a rule of thumb, an educated guess, an intuitive judgment, stereotyping, profiling, or apportioning wealth for a favorable personal return.

This reality is troubling because Assyrians of average median income would be able to generate more revenue because they number more than wealthy individuals by population. However, the Assyrians classified in the median income group are reluctant to donate to one cause because of the lack of democratic and transparent donation processes in Assyrian fundraising, thus causing a lack of uniformity of financial donations to Assyrian organizations and generating insufficient results. Furthermore, because Assyrians at the average median income level have a low capital reserve, the risks are greater because the cost of donating may hinder the standard of living, and the rewards from contribution are minor.

Globalization

Globalization is rapidly converging economies and governments even though substantial inequalities between rich and poor countries remain.[246] Globalization is the process by which markets are integrated worldwide, causing countries to become interdependent upon each other to sustain and maintain growth in their economies.[247] Today, a "collapse in one state's stock market can trigger rapid meltdowns in other markets." Destructive computer viruses can spread in hours or days. And "carbon emissions in the United States and China" can "change sea levels in the Netherlands or cause increasingly severe and unpredictable weather around the globe."[248]

---

[244] Gerd Gigerenzer. How to Make Cognitive Delusions Disappear: Beyond Heuristic Biases. Oxford: European Review of Social Psychology, 1991. pg. 83-115. Print.
[245] Ibid.
[246] Thomas Piketty. Capital in the Twenty-First Century. P.261
[247] Michael Spence. "The Impact of Globalization on Income and Employment." Foreign Affairs (2011). Print.
[248] Rosa Brooks. "Crafting a Progressive Foreign Policy in Today's World." Progressivism in America.

The realities of the emerging global economy are shaping how Assyrians respond to the consequences of globalization. Assyrians do not have a state; therefore, they must conform to their respective domicile's market, trade, and industry. Until about three decades ago, globalization had minimal effects on the distribution of wealth and jobs. But as developing countries, where most Assyrians do not reside, became larger and richer, their economic structures began to produce high-value commercial components that 30 years ago were only of exclusive attention among advanced economies.

This change in economics is perpetual and inevitable. With China and India accounting for 40 percent of the world's population, these structural changes will only have a greater impact on the world's future. Globalization has been affecting the price of goods, job patterns, and wages. It is changing the structure of individual economies in ways that affect different groups within those countries differently.[249] In the advanced economies, globalization is redistributing employment opportunities and incomes. An example of the effects of globalization to a certain group would be Assyrians domiciled in America. The United States is home to the third-largest population of Assyrians around the world.[250] Although the US census in 2010 counted 110,807 Assyrians in the United States, the unofficial estimated amount was 400,000 and will most likely rise, considering the chaos in Assyrians' native region. Nearly all Assyrians living in America who are eligible for employment seek occupational tasks. However, these tasks have been difficult to complete in America.

Because of economic policy responding to globalization, many job opportunities in the United States are shifting away from economic

Oxford University Press. (2016)
[249] Ibid.
[250] "American Factfinder" US Census.gov. (October 2013)

sectors experiencing the most growth and are moving toward countries that are less developed. The result is growing disparities in income and employment across the US economy, with "highly educated workers enjoying more opportunities and workers with less education facing declining employment prospects and stagnant incomes." The presumed problem of America's "declining competitiveness" would be blamed for much of what seemed to ail America, including the stagnation of the average American's income.[251] "Certain American industries that once dominated world commerce … have lost much of their market share both at home and abroad; in a few industries … the American presence in the market has all but disappeared."[252] Therefore, American corporations or industries are ceasing to exist in any form that can meaningfully be distinguished from the rest of the global economy. For that matter, the American economy as a whole is "not retaining a distinct identity; Americans succeed or fail together. Thus, the standard of living for Americans, as well as of the citizens of other nations, core corporations, and industries, demand their skills and insights."[253]

This evolving structure of the global economy demonstrates that the ambitions and goals concerning Assyrians may be obstructed because globalization has diverse effects on different groups of people. Opportunities are expanding only for the highly educated throughout the economy, and the majority of the Assyrian population in the United States, although proceeding to education, still face uncertainty in a globalized economy. Furthermore, "opportunities are expanding for those who are well educated, but opportunities are shrinking for the less well educated."[254] The highly specialized educated will be able to benefit from globalization in that it will expose individuals to innovation.[255] "The internet has expanded the ability to communicate with each other, improving both access to knowledge and the possible range of contacts."[256] Therefore, unless the generation of Assyrians

---

[251] Michael Spence. Foreign Affairs. (2011)
[252] M. Dertouzos, R. Lester, R. Solow, et al., Made in America: Regaining the Productive Edge (Cambridge: MIT Press, 1989)
[253] Work of Nations. P. 77
[254] Ibid.
[255] Joseph Stiglitz. Creating a Learning Society. P. 61 Columbia University Press. New York. 2014
[256] Ibid.

born in the United States and other Western countries (millennials) retain a highly specialized educational skill, then globalization may hinder financial donations to the Assyrian cause.

Assyrians cannot bar the timelessness and importance of a highly specialized education. Such an education includes "symbolic-analytical services, such as problem solving, problem identifying, and strategic brokering activities."[257] Symbolic analysts "solve, identify, and broker problems by manipulating symbols, simplifying reality into abstract images that can be rearranged, juggled, experimented with, communicated to other specialists, and then eventually transformed back into reality."[258] The manipulations are done with analytic tools and are sharpened by experiences. The tools may be "mathematical algorithms, legal arguments, financial gimmicks, scientific principles, psychological insights into how to persuade or to amuse, systems of inductions or deductions, or any other set of techniques for solving conceptual puzzles."[259]

Symbolic analysts often work alone or in small teams, which may be connected to larger organizations. Teamwork is often critical because "neither problems nor solutions can be defined in advance. Frequent, and informal conversations help ensure that insights and discoveries are put to their best uses and subjected to quick, critical evaluation."[260] This will help lead Assyrians to enter occupations such as doctors, lawyers, design engineers, civil engineers, architects, pharmacists, executive managers, investment bankers, and computer scientists. Also included is the amount of work done by "management consultants, informational specialists, advertising executives, art directors, cinematographers, film editors, publishers, writers, editors, journalists, musicians, television and film producers, and even university professors."[261] These occupations will help alleviate the effects of the emerging twenty-first century global economy that bears only a superficial resemblance to prior global economies.

---

[257] Ibid. P. 78
[258] Ibid. pp.79-80
[259] Ibid. pp.90-91
[260] Work of Nations. P. 179
[261] Work of Nations. P. 178

Further, occupations previously mentioned will help Assyrian professionals to have a secure standard of living without falling victim to the risk of losing a job overseas. In the United States, "the steel, plastic, high-tech, and telecommunications industry have managed to maintain high profits but have specialized their industry to particular uses."[262] Therefore, the new barrier for individual groups such as Assyrians will be to find the skill and expertise to specialize and perform symbolic analysts services. This has motivated industry to rely on a "high-valued business to help drive them forward and not a high-volume business."[263] In order to help understand what skills are required, one must discern what is valuable to certain industries.

According to former United States Secretary of Labor Robert B. Reich, there are three characteristics of valuable skills that are relevant to retaining a symbolic analyst position. First are the problem-solving skills required to put things together in unique ways. Problem solvers must have intimate knowledge of what such things might be able to do and create signs and instructions for facilitating such outcomes. Unlike the researchers and designers whose "prototypes" emerged fully from a "laboratory or drafting table ready for high-volume productions, these people are involved in the continuing search for new applications, combinations, and refinements capable of solving sorts of emerging problems."[264]

Next are the skills required to help customers or clients understand their needs and how customized products or services can meet those needs. In contrast with selling and marketing standardized goods—which requires "persuading many customers of the virtues of one particular product, taking lots of orders for it, and thus meeting sales quotas—selling and marketing customized products and services requires having intimate knowledge of the customer or client's business or industry." This intimate knowledge may "induce a competitive advantage because of new problems and possibilities; therefore, the art of persuasion is replaced by the identification of

---

262 Ibid.
263 Work of Nations. P. 84
264 Work of Nations. pp. 84-85

opportunity."[265]

Third are the skills needed to "link problem solvers and problem identifiers." People in such roles must understand enough about specific technologies and markets to see the potential in new services or products, raise whatever money is necessary to launch the project, and assemble the right problem solvers and identifiers to carry it out. Those occupying this position are called "executives" or "entrepreneurs." These people are "continuously engaged in managing the ideas of a strategic broker."[266]

These three factors are vital because of the potential opportunity to future Assyrian generations but will also help reciprocate personal influence and alleviate the threat of globalization within the Assyrian global community. In a sense, it permits an individual Assyrian to become a "cosmopolitan." A cosmopolitan is one who is familiar and at ease with many different cultures and countries. Prospectively, then their personal influence may be compounded by their tendency to agree with one another on critical Assyrian issues. This will not cause a conspiracy or collusion but rather create the consequence of having shared many of the same formal experiences and gained many of the same perspectives along the way. Perhaps by attending the "same universities, studying the same discipline, enduring the difficulties of performance deadlines", navigating bureaucracies, "reading the same social media outlet, belonging to the same clubs or unions, vacationing at the same resorts."[267] This type of planning may bring solidarity because of common experiences in a small community that lacks amity within itself. Thus, solidarity between the millennials may entice a predisposed intrinsic core for regional political integration and international cooperation.

---

[265] Ibid. P.84-85
[266] Ibid. P. 85
[267] Fortune, July 1957. P. 94

CHAPTER ELEVEN – REGIONAL POLITICAL INTEGRATION

Regional political integration means to incorporate, consolidate, and merge political organizations together wherever situated. The ultimate goal would be to have one, as many as two, political parties on a united platform toward Assyrian development. These organizations may operate as separate entities but must incorporate by reference their goals, funds, and objectives within each organization. Regional integration may be able to pool together a collective action by sharing financial information and cultivating a pool of resources that may be withdrawn when readily needed. However, the counterargument concerning this recommendation is that integration will undermine the existing goals of each organization, thus becoming counterproductive to Assyrian progression. This argument is not compelling because all organizations have the same foundation to assist Assyrians around the world; therefore, how would consolidating the resources of each organization undermine the objectives of helping Assyrians? Organizations may pursue matters despite a concurrent conflict of interest if there is reasonable belief parties can proceed with diligence and competence without adversely limiting actions.

Furthermore, because integration is a new idea, the integration would require aid in formulation of a new ideology rather than maintain the traditional status quo. In other words, Assyrian groups around the world would have to simultaneously abide by the new belief of a national idea of patriotism and economic unity. There must be a system within an Assyrian organization that espouses a set of more or less persistent integrated doctrines that purport to explain and justify leadership.[268]   One reason why leaders develop an ideology is to "endow their leadership with legitimacy, to convert their political influence into authority, and eventually justify the whole political ideology itself."[269]   This ideology is then the official belief of the political system because the moral, religious, and factual assumptions

---

[268] Robert Dahl. What is Politics: Modern Political Analysis. Prentice Hall Publishers. 1963 P. 54
[269] Ibid.

are assumed to justify the official ideology controlling the political system, thus facilitating a comprehensive scheme or plan that would pre-empt any organization from hindering the political system's intentions. This ideology must concern Assyrian development through democratic principles and transparency.

The prerequisite for the ideology of change is "possession of basic truth."[270] Currently, the basic truth regarding Assyrians is the fact that Assyrians are enduring a resource dilemma precluding progression. Also, another basic truth is that the world is changing and everything is both interrelated and fluctuating. Therefore, Assyrian development must be "loose, resilient, and fluid to the extent that organizations integrating and cooperating can respond to the realities of the widely different cultures and societies" of the Middle East. Further, the organization and its organizer must have "conviction, a belief that if people have the power to act, in the long run they will reach the right decisions."[271]

The basic requirement for the understanding of the basic truth of the Assyrian resource dilemma and alleviating the burden of change is to recognize the world as it is. Assyrians must work with it on its terms if we are to change it to the kind of world that is favorable to Assyrians. For example, the prime misconception in regards to the status quo of Assyrian organizations is based on the false belief that components working within one organization are separate from their inevitable counterparts. However, one knows intellectually that everything is functionally interrelated, but, in Assyrian resource operations, Assyrian organizations segment and isolate themselves from one another. "The long-term results of being isolated is that [groups] provide members with a means to feel like they're involved in change, but the involvement is highly individualistic and confined largely to acts of symbolic solidarity."[272]

---

[270] Saul Alinksy. Rules for Radicals. Vintage Books. 1971. P. 10
[271] Ibid. P. 12
[272] Vivek, Chibber. The Twentieth Century Left Socialists Plenty of Lessons. Will We Heed them? Jacobin. The First Red Century. No 27 Fall 2017.

Assyrian organizations must see life in its duality. In other words, in the world as it is, the solution of each problem inevitably creates a new one. The grasp of the duality of all "phenomena is vital in our understanding of politics. It frees one from the myth that one approach is positive and another negative. There is no such thing in life."[273] One man's positive is another man's negative. The Assyrian organizations and their organizers must be acceptable to the global Assyrian population by "demonstrating competence, talent, and courage, because when people have a genuine opportunity to act and to change conditions they'll begin to think their problems through."[274] Assyrian organizations must serve as a protective shield to the Assyrian global population. If anything goes wrong, it is the entire organization's fault. If the organizations are successful, then all credit goes to the local population that helped accomplish the success.

The Assyrian organization must know and be sensitive to the shadows that surround it, and one shadow is getting the majority of the Assyrian population to understand the new idea of regional political integration and cooperation. Rationalization of a new idea can be accomplished by emphasizing to the Assyrian population the inefficiency of the status quo. Further, stressing the notion that change through political integration and cooperation will come power, and power comes from organization. In order to "act, people must act together."[275] Giving the Assyrian global population, an idea of power is not enough; Assyrian organizations have to allow the Assyrian global population to experience this idea in action. The organization's job is to begin to build confidence and hope in the idea of organization and, thus, in the Assyrian people themselves. Simultaneously, the Assyrian organization carries on many functions as it analyzes, attacks, and disrupts the prevailing power pattern.

A new ideology would require inducing apathetic Assyrians to participate because more resources are needed. The new ideology should be based on a democratic and transparent Assyria that is not related to pre-existing obligations to established Assyrian organization.

---

273 Rules for Radicals. P. 106
274 Rules for Radicals. P. 17
275 Rules for Radicals. P.113

Each organization may be split into different tasks, such as security, humanitarian aid, political representation, economic support, and administrative tasks, and all the donations to each organization would be pooled together and appropriated toward the necessity. In order to achieve this, the organization's membership should be proportional to the Assyrian population globally. This will enable the organizations to regain control of disseminating a universal message of Assyrian progress—not just to Assyrian leaders but also to Assyrian citizens living in the Diaspora. The means to achieve integration would be to incorporate the tactics of Assyrian humanitarian aid, security forces, and volunteer tourism organized particularly to help illustrate the Assyrian resource dilemma.

Political integration will require neutrality toward religion when pursuing a decided action. One may argue that if Assyrian Church of the East will be integrated politically, the historical precedent of Church leaders providing political leadership will continue causing no integration or counterproductive integration. This argument is not true because history has demonstrated as with Europe, Israel and the United States it is possible to develop a secular state while simultaneously adhering to a faith-based religion.

In order to achieve harmony between church and political organizations, all integration decisions should be found invalid unless the action has a "secular purpose"; has a "primary effect that neither advances nor inhibits religion"; and "integration decisions do not produce excessive entanglement with religion."[276] This protocol will help screen decision-making without undue delay because the procedure prevents preference of one religious sect over the Assyrian Nation. For example, this process will prevent financial aid to religiously or unconnected affiliated organizations operating within the integration. The resource developed by the integration must be contributed for and be disbursed to a defined class of persons as long as the class is defined without reference to religion or religious criteria and the decision favors a large segment of Assyrians. Political integration is plausible and can lead to effective decision-making if there is cooperation between Assyrians.

---

[276] Lemon v. Kurtzman, 403 U.S.US 602 (1971) – the "Lemon" test

Among all Assyrians focused on Assyrian progression, there must be solidarity and authority mutuality between these groups. Unless things change, it is difficult to imagine a lasting solution to the Assyrian resource dilemma, thus precluding an opportunity to establish a nation state. In an ideal system, all the donations and finance declarations by secular and church groups would pool their resources accumulated for the specific purpose of building an "Assyria fund." Granted, the Assyrian Church of the East would not pool all of its resources, considering it must spread the gospels. However, because the church has accumulated more wealth than any political organization representing Assyrians, it would not hinder progression if coupled with secular support and proportionality, if fairly apportioned. The protocol for the system must be democratic and transparent. In order to ensure a democratic and open system, there must be a courtroom aspect to every process.

Every Assyrian needs to genuinely and sincerely participate in the modern debate of the struggle for Assyrians in a responsible and professional manner without spontaneous claims that cannot be corroborated with empirical or reliable circumstantial evidence. Therefore, participation must be guided by a set of rules and standards by which admissions of proof are regulated during the decision-making process. The material facts in the decision must be determined by proof that is filtered through testimony, writings, and physical evidence. This process will prevent certain individuals from participating who are likely to base decisions that appeal to emotions or are reactionary instead of proactive, thus obstructing the true intentions of Assyrian development.

Actual and documentary evidence must be authenticated as accurate and reliable by a neutral or exhausted source, and opinions should be based on facts within one's personal knowledge. Knowledge must be relevant, reliably based on accurate principals, and based on reasonable probability regarding the opinion; the topic opined must be based on scientific, technical, or other specialized knowledge.

Therefore, those presenting evidence must be experts within the opinion given. However, the difference between "opinion" and "fact" is a matter of degree. For that reason, one who is not an expert may offer testimony when it rationally based on the perception of the witness and, helpful to the decision-making process, even if it is not based on scientific, technical, or other specialized knowledge.

The decision-making process will be assigned to representatives based on territory within the diaspora. Therefore, each region where a substantial amount of Assyrians are located would have a representative acting for their best interest. The representatives would be fiduciaries of their region, which means they must act with reasonable care and the utmost loyalty to the Assyrians they represent. The duty of care means that the agent would act as a reasonable prudent person under similar circumstances, and the duty of loyalty infers that the representative must not usurp power for his own interest, or adversely and materially limit representation because of a conflicting interest. Furthermore, to ensure transparency, this process must not be done secretly but with full disclosure to the Assyrian people, regardless of the policy initiated. If this is accomplished, then it is possible for Assyrians to construct a continental political authority capable of reasserting trust and legitimacy over all Assyrians in the twenty-first century. Finally, these organizations may bring a sense of legitimate authority within the Assyrian community and become a revolving door for educated, articulate Assyrians who wish to form the apparition of Assyria into a reality.

CHAPTER TWELVE – INTERNATIONAL COOPERATION

International cooperation between Assyrians in the diaspora is essential to help solve the Assyrian resource dilemma. International cooperation asks what policies and institutions will bring us together as a nation. The first policy would encourage all Assyrians to contribute based on their skill, knowledge, or expertise. The second policy would be account for every donation and expenditure in a database that is accessible to every Assyrian who contributed. The counterargument is that democracy cannot be achieved through international cooperation because Assyria is not a state; therefore, it cannot utilize democratic characteristics. However, cynicism would render such an idea as utopian. These arguments fade in importance compared to Assyrians' need for accurate representation that reflects their lives and the totality of their circumstances. Moreover, international cooperation will require a large number of Assyrians that are dissimilarly and similarly situated to address consistent ideas, theories, and claims. International cooperation will not require that all organizations come to an agreement because the characteristics of international cooperation are broad. The only certain characteristic would be democracy; agreement is not essential in a democracy but participation is.

Another reason why Assyrians could do with structured cooperation is to encourage participation by precluding indifference. Precluding indifference within the Assyrian global community would maximize its potential and avail Assyrians of all the skills and knowledge each individual Assyrian has. Apathetic Assyrians regard nationalism as "removing themselves as actual citizens of a nation seeking an independent state and remand themselves with the complacent role of political commentator or critically demolish the aspirations, views,"[277] and performance of optimistic Assyrians. It would be "erroneous to think that there are separate worlds"[278] between those Assyrians devoting their energy to Assyria, those that are commentators, and those that are complacent, apathetic Assyrians

---

[277] Thomas Piketty. Capital in the Twenty-First Century. P. 585
[278] Ibid.

in the diaspora. Apathy poses dangerous risks because those Assyrians assuming authority rely on "immoderate use of theories and ideas, which, if not examined thoroughly, will be utilized merely to justify inefficient policies or mask the emptiness of the status quo." Apathy causes too much "energy to be exhausted on pure assumption without a clear measurement of adequate facts or objectives explaining the rationale behind the policies."[279]

To overcome the struggle of the diaspora, Assyrians around the world must work together as a nation in order to gain political consolidation and global cooperation from every Assyrian around the globe. The idea of political consolidation and global cooperation between Assyrians will pose difficulty because of cultural internal issues. "What each individual believes is affected by what others believe. Further, the prisms through which we see the world are largely socially determined, called pre-confirmatory bias."[280] Pre-confirmatory biases tend to exhibit "irrational exuberance" which hinders innovative ideas by overestimating, or underestimating externalities that may affect leadership decisions.[281] Thus, removing biases as much as possible may alleviate making inferences and assumptions that affect prior beliefs that "may discount information which is inconsistent with the bias and to accept information that is consistent with those beliefs."[282]

---

[279] Thomas Piketty. Capital in the Twenty-First Century. P. 586
[280] Joseph Stiglitz. Creating a Learning Society. Columbia University Press. New York 2014.
[281] Ibid.
[282] Ibid.

Cooperation can be possible if Assyrian ethos is transformed from a shame society to a guilt culture. A shame culture is a society in which the primary device for gaining "control over children and maintaining social order is the inculcation of shame and the complementary threat of ostracism."[283] A guilt culture is a society in which the primary method of social control in a society is the "inculcation of feelings of guilt for behaviors that the individual believes to be undesirable."[284] Both guilt and shame culture rely on internalized convictions of bad and good. However, shame culture emphasizes "ridicule and ostracism from other people", whereas guilt culture "emphasizes punishment and forgiveness as ways of restoring moral order."[285]

Transitioning Assyrian culture to a guilt society may seem difficult, considering the discrepancy between immigrant Assyrians from the Middle East living in the Western world and first-born generation Assyrians that have adopted Western notions of democratic and transparent ideas. The traditional Assyrians currently assume leadership and adhere to a shame culture, but the later first-born Assyrians represent the millennial generation that will be prone to abide by a guilt culture.

---

[283] Ruth Benedict (1989). The Chrysanthemum and the Sword: Patterns of Japanese Culture.
[284] Ibid.
[285] Ibid.

Millennials are those who were born between 1980 and 2000s. As of 2018, the first cohort of millennial are in their early 30s and pose a more vital use for Assyrians because they are better familiar with Western societies from their experience and logic with technology, and investing in human capital such as education and training. Millennials also value "community, family, and innovation and are the largest, most diverse group in America."[286] For example, an Assyrian–American millennial is an educated or experienced young professional who still values Assyrian tradition while simultaneously familiarizing him or her with other culturally relevant societies, whereas the traditional generation is complacent with society if that society offers safety and habitability.

Discrepancies between generations will not last, however, because the traditional generation has been outperformed by the millennial generation because of contemporary opportunities to gain knowledge and expertise offered in democracies such as America, Canada, European countries, and Australia. These internal factors of social mobility will overcome the traditional powers to forego past tribal conflicts and political debates that have hindered Assyrian progression. What the present Assyrian generation wants is what all democratic generations have always wanted—a meaning, a sense of what the world and life are, and a chance to strive for some sort of order.

Although the generational discrepancy is not perpetual, it is important that both generations converge together as soon as possible to reassure that a united Assyrian population is assembling. Assyrians today obtain a great deal of skill and knowledge in different disciplines that will benefit Assyrian progression. If the first-born generations in the Western world mobilized as successors with interest in traditional organizations but with a new effective approach for Assyrian progression, this would symbolize constructive progression because a successor in interest is one who is willing to commit to a common cause established by a predecessor.

---

[286] 15 Economic facts about Millennials. The Council of Economic Advisors (October 2014). Retrieved August 1, 2015.

Along with the modifications to the organizations, traditional Assyrians must demonstrate eagerness to induce the younger generation of Assyrians born in the Western world to become successors in interest. Any attempts to restrict a successor in interest from millennial generations would detract from the Assyrian cause because it may preclude confidence and hope regarding future innovative Assyrian development. One counterargument by those who currently exercise power is that organizations such as Zowaa or the Assyrian Universal Alliance have modified themselves to conform to the changes of the world and have induced many young followers toward their cause, which may be partially true. However, this argument may not be valid because if organizations were modified to commit to a more democratic and transparent protocol of resource development, one might ask why Assyrians would be in such dire circumstances as they were 100 years ago in the same region. Further, if these organizations have reformed themselves, then why are Assyrians experiencing successive frustrations to the point that the desire to participate has seemed to atrophy because the method for raising money for Assyrians in the Middle East has succumbed to redundant inefficient causes that spend a great deal of their time explaining the means to the end or justifying their work as the only relevant means to an end. Assyrians must implement a national bargain of sacrificing that consists of patriotism by each Assyrian, regional political integration by political organizations, and international cooperation on the part of each Assyrian facet contributing to Assyrian progression.

However, progression cannot be achieved if leaders and supporters of secular movements criticize the Assyrian Church of the East Relief Organization (ACERO) because it is divisive within an environment of scare resource. ACERO, by numbers, has more followers than these organizations because of its longstanding tradition. Acknowledged, ACERO's purpose is not germane to set up a military or common defense because it conflicts with its interest in spreading worship and gospel. However, ACERO does apply to diplomacy because of its legitimate authority within the Assyrian community. Therefore, it is not within Assyria's interest for political organizations to criticize ACERO's practice of diplomacy. ACERO must, however, recuse itself from secular decision-making while concurrently giving these organizations their blessing and financial support to present a united front on all levels of the Assyrian people, thus demonstrating unanimity of collective passion.

SECTION V—QUESTIONS REGARDING SUSTAINABILITY FOR ASSYRIAN PROGRESSION

CHAPTER THIRTEEN – ASSYRIAN SUSTAINABILITY

To summarize, The Assyrian population is enduring a resource dilemma from a totality of unfortunate global circumstances. One element of circumstance is Assyrian organizations contributing to depleting resources by competition for funds causing resources to be scarce within a small community, therefore precluding efficient Assyrian development. The mechanism to solve the resource dilemma in Assyrian politics is based on an Assyrian national bargain to learn democratic and transparent process of accumulating resources for Assyrian development. Subjecting Assyrian organizations to democratic and transparent procedures requires the Assyrian global population to accept the authority that induces political integration and international cooperation by Assyrian organizations and leaders.

According to German political economist Max Weber, "politics is the sharing of power between various groups, and political leaders are those who wield this power."[287] In Weber's most influential contributions, Politics as a Vocation, Weber discusses that authority is power accepted as legitimate by those subjected to it. Therefore, leaders try to ensure that whatever means are used to deal with conflict, the decisions arrived at are widely accepted not solely from fear of violence, punishment, or coercion but from a belief that is morally right and proper to do so.[288] Leaders are said to be legitimate if the people to whom its orders are directed believe that "the structure, procedures, acts, decisions, policies, officials, or leaders possess the quality of "rightness," propriety, or moral goodness."[289] Then, because of the "rightness," the acquisition of legitimacy transcends into authority. Three ideal types of political leadership appear in the hierarchal development order: charismatic authority, traditional authority, and legal authority.

---

[287] Daniel Warner (1991). An Ethic of Responsibility in International Relations. Lynne Rienner Publishers. pp. 9–10. Retrieved 5 April 2011.
[288] Robert Dahl. What is Politics: Modern Political Analysis. Prentice Hall Publishers. 1963 P. 54
[289] Ibid.

Charismatic authority stems from a charismatic leader having a dynamic personality by applying extraordinary qualities and exceptional powers that accomplish success within the community. These leaders are emotionally unstable and volatile, and once the charismatic leader dies, process of turning into a rational democracy will begin.

Traditional authority stems from a dominant personal leader that has been established by tradition or routine and acquired or inherited his qualities. Traditional followers are based on allegiance of feeling of a common purpose and established forms of social conduct.

Legal rational authority is a functional superior or bureaucratic official having established authority by virtue of rationally established norms, decrees, rules, and regulators. The general belief within a rational legal system is the formal correctness of these rules and those who enact this are considered a legitimized authority. Superiors are subject to rules that "limit their powers, separate their private lives from official duties and require documentation."[290]

Applying Weber's construction, the Assyrian leadership has interrelated his ideals of authority, particularly, traditional authority and charismatic authority with the former being the more dominate authority utilized by Assyrian organizations. An organizations' acquisition of legitimacy is vital to maintain authority for Assyrian development. For that reason, it is essential to address numerous questions regarding their sustainability of authority in order to transcend that authority to a legal rational authority that is adequately functioning.

First, funds must be donated in a democratic and transparent manner to reassure donors that their money is being funded for the groups' primary purposes. This means that every donation should be accounted for and every dollar should be counted and revealed on an open forum or website database for every Assyrian in the world to empirically locate. This will ensure confidence and stability through

---

[290] Reinhard Bendix, Max Weber: An Intellectual Portrait, University of California Press, 1977, P. 294

democratic principles because, as Weber stated, authority is power that is legitimate to those subjected to it. An Assyrian, whether highly educated or not, would recognize the legitimacy of an organization applying democratic and transparent principles.

Second, the tardiness of Assyrian militias suggests that Assyrian leaders have lacked capability and resources to develop Assyrian security in Iraq. Setting up a common defense for a group of indigenous minorities in a heavily divided region of the world should be the first undertaking and commitment achieved by an operating political organization. The fact that the Nineveh Protection Unit (NPU) was created in 2014, over a decade after the war in Iraq, implies that Assyrian leadership either did not have the resources to commit to such a cause or did not have the capacity to consider the chaotic effects of a war-torn country. A military defense has always existed and overlaps traditional and rational legal authority. Thus, the NPU and its leaders must demonstrate a significant drive toward a rational legal rule through democratic protocols and transparency and be supported by proper documentation.

As noted earlier, the only consistent trend in Iraq is a chaotic transition to democracy, which stagnates Iraq as a quasi-anarchic state, particularly in areas of northern Iraq. This lack of superior administration, ruling, and governing within the state structure of Iraq (quasi-anarchy) enforces already "existing mutual mistrust by creating additional security concerns for many groups that have experienced past discrimination."[291] A quasi-anarchic state, however, creates a chaotic society "impossible to carry out democratic elections, try cases at court, design or enforce laws, or manage quiet business of government."[292] Thus, "agencies besides the state also have access to violence. People and parties who wish to undermine democracy and rule of law create and fund violent organizations that involve themselves in politics."[293] Such groups can "take the form of a parliamentary wing of political party, the personal bodyguard of a particular politician or apparently spontaneous citizens' initiatives, which usually turn out to have been organized for an ulterior motive."[294]

---

[291] Verena, Gruber. Revisiting Civil-Military-Relations Theory - The Case of the Kurdish Regional Government of Iraq. Master's thesis, Lund University, 2015. Lund, Sweden: Verena Gruber, 2015

[292] Ibid.

[293] Timothy, Snyder. On Tyranny: Twenty lessons from the twentieth century. New York: Tim Duggan Books, 2017.

[294] Ibid.

Armed groups may "degrade political order, create a climate of fear and then transform it."[295] Paramilitaries may use force against "dissenter and dilute those expressing different opinions." Therefore it is essential that armed guards be "reflective of their goals."[296] Reflection of armed guards should be based on "human evils of the past that involved armed guards and soldiers finding themselves doing irregular things, and a reflective person is prepared to say no to irregular tasks."[297] Without reflection of past evils, "soldiers or armed guards may find themselves in an unknown land conforming to murder without any special preparation." Therefore, paramilitaries may induce tyranny within the Assyrian population to demonstrate strength and accumulate resources that should be devoted to other causes than just the funding of violence.

The creation of a protection force would not have endured the same burdens in 2003 as the NPU faces in the present day. In 2003, ISIL did not have the power to achieve its brutal objectives. Furthermore, the fundamental worldview for Assyrians should have been focused on defending the Assyrian interest. Any legitimate political organizations would acknowledge the need for a common defense after the invasion on Iraq; therefore, the NPU came later than expected to most Assyrians. Although these questions must be entertained to prevent another late push for Assyrian progression, they must not be the primary focus because it will create a disbelieving worldview of pessimism in the Assyrian community, and pessimism is a luxury an Assyrian can never enjoy.

---

[295] Ibid.
[296] Ibid.
[297] Ibid.

Third, will the procedures of these organizations be sufficient to overcome an Assyrian resource dilemma? This question bears the analysis of how Assyrians will consolidate and change their interests to accumulate the most resources for Assyrian development. All change means disorganization of the old and organization of the new. Therefore, new ideas toward current Assyrian organizations will be immediately confronted with conflict. The organizer dedicated to changing the life of a particular community must first rub raw the resentments of the people of the community and fan out the latent hostilities of many of the people to the point of overt expression. Organizations must search out issues, rather than avoid them, for unless there is controversy people are not concerned enough to act.[298] Organizations must "provide a channel into which the people can angrily pour their frustrations."[299]

This process seems difficult and burdensome, considering the totality of circumstances regarding Assyrians; however, one must recognize that nothing will be accomplished unless Assyrians mobilize on their own. Lobbying action for a safe haven will be futile if Assyrians cannot maintain their own freedom, administrative functions, and economic stability.[300] One must not presume that Assyrian development is a utopian proposal because the idea is no more utopian than a restructuring of politics of the Middle East established after World War II. Therefore, it is essential to research and draw analogies of Israel and Palestine with the current Assyrian struggles.

---

[298] Rules for Radicals. P. 116

[299] Rules for Radicals. P. 117

[300] According to Wikileaks Cable: 08BAGHDAD1830_a, Christian IDPs expressed great skepticism about an autonomous zone in a dinner meeting with NEA-I Director June 11, noting it would become like Israel, surrounded by enemies. They said it would "isolate Christians from their Iraqi heritage and homeland, and that the communities they now live in would push them to live with their own brethren in the autonomous zone." They asked "what would we do, stuck in small villages in the Nineveh Plain?" Many Christian IDPs are professionals, engineers and medical doctors, reluctant to build up their lives in small villages, where agriculture would likely be the primary occupation. The Christian IDPs expressed gratefulness to Minister Sarkis and the KRG, as they have offered protection for Christians, and recognized their plight while the Government of Iraq offers nothing.

CHAPTER FOURTEEN – COMMINALITES AND DIFFERENCES WITH ISRAEL/PALESTINE

It is important to note that Assyrians, Arabs, and Israelis are Semitic people in terms of cultural heritage, history, and identity. The term Semitic refers to studies of linguistics and ethnology to refer to a family of people derived from the Middle East. Biblically, a Semite derives from Shem, one of the three sons of Noah. For Assyrians and Hebrews, in an effort to categorize the peoples known to them, those closest to them in culture and language were generally deemed to be descended from their supposed forefather Shem.[301]   Therefore, Assyrians, Arabs, and Israelis are linked together through their Semitic culture.

Coupled with a Semitic identity, both Assyrians and Israelis have commonalities of being oppressed because of their existence in the Middle East region. The motivation for the oppression is because both cultures have practiced a religion that is not Islam. Furthermore, throughout the past centuries, Arab, Turkish, Kurdish, and Persian demographics that practice Islam substantially outnumbered both Assyrian and Israeli populations. These similar characteristics have the same discriminatory effects for both non-Islamic cultures which are underrepresented and therefore overlooked.

Similar to Assyrians, the Israeli people have endured historic oppression. For example, the Israelis experienced the notorious Holocaust of WWII subsequently after the genocide of the Assyrians during the Great War. Furthermore, both the Assyrians and Israelis have survived a diaspora. However, there is a major difference between Israelis and Assyrians in the twenty-first century, because Israel has a state and Assyrians are without state.

---

[301] Two of Shem's sons were Assur (Assyrian descent) and Arphaxad (Israeli descent)

According to PBS's *A Royal Tour of Israel*, Egypt, Syria, Jordan, and Lebanon, with Saudi Arabia directly to the southwest, border the small state of Israel. "Israel has always been in conflict-prone vicinity. Israel was created on May 14, 1948, when a UN resolution set aside land as an official Jewish State, which was formerly under British control."[302] For Israelis, their new nation was "more than just a refuge from persecution; it was a return to the homeland that they believed had originally been theirs."[303] Now Israelis are rebuilding their homeland to a great rebirth of the Jewish people. However, "peace has been elusive, as Israel has fought several wars against Arab coalitions, with the most significant being the Six Day War of 1967."[304] After a peace treaty, with Israel relinquishing all that was gained after the Six Day War, Israel continued to progress despite much resentment within the Middle East.

The similarities between Israelis and Assyrians are genocide, dwindling population, and misperceptions of the interpretations of their people. Similarly, both cultures breed and yearn for peace; both cultures greet each other with "peace."[305] Finally, the sense of irredentism, which is the ambition to gain control of native land that was lost by another group, is as prevalent among Assyrians as instilled in Israelis. Assyrians wish to gain control of northern Iraq and the southeastern part of Syria, while Israel sought to free the land of Palestine. These commonalities of seeking peace and regaining former land are two parallel worldviews between both cultures.

---

[302] Israel: The Royal Tour. PBS, 2014. DVD.
[303] Ibid.
[304] Jeremy Bowen (2003). Six Days: How the 1967 War Shaped the Middle East. London: Simon & Schuster.
[305] Shalom means peace in Hebrew. Shalma means peace in Assyrian

One must discern the Israeli process of democratization from the Assyrian process. First, the timing between the creation of Israel and Assyria must be distinguished. Israel was created after the holocaust and two major world wars. Granted, the Assyrians endured similar misery, but denial and World War II superseded recognition of the Assyrian Genocide. The reasons for superseding the Assyrian genocide are based on the idea that Assyrians are rarely studied, rarely researched, rarely known, and usually reduced to "Christians" or a euphemism that leads to Assyrians being generalized as Christian Arabs or Kurds. Thus generalization and reduction of Assyrian culture leads to the "recapitulation of orientalism."[306]

Orientalism is the "humanistic study of patronizing perceptions and fictional depictions of the Middle East, i.e., the societies and peoples who inhabit the places of...the East."[307] Patronizing the Orient is accomplished through four dogmas: "one is the absolute and systematic difference between the West, which is rational, developed, humane, superior, and the Orient (Middle East) which is aberrant, undeveloped, inferior." Another dogma is that "abstractions through texts by Westerners about the Orient are preferable in representing the Middle East than actual Oriental realties." A third dogma is that the Orient is "eternal, uniform, and incapable of defining itself; therefore, a Western standpoint for describing the Middle East is inevitable." Fourth is that the Orient is at the "bottom," thus "something either to be feared or to be controlled."[308]

---

[306] Natasha Norman. August 22, 2006 article depicts Assyrian woman named Babylonia as a "Kurdish Christian fighting ISIL.
[307] The New Fontana Dictionary of Modern Thought, Third Edition. (1999) p. 617.
[308] Edward Said. Orientalism. Vintage Books. New York. 1979. P. 300-301

Orientalism proposes that much of Western study of the Middle East was an exercise in political intellectualism, a psychological exercise in the self-affirmation of "European identity," and not an "objective exercise of intellectual enquiry and the academic study of Eastern cultures." Therefore, Orientalism was a method of "practical and cultural discrimination, which was applied to non-European societies and peoples in order to establish European imperial domination." In justification of the empire, the Orientalist claims to know "more—essential and definitive knowledge—about the Orient than do the Orientals."[309]

Because of Orientalism, the world's economy, power, and ideas have supported Israel significantly since the time Israel was created. Furthermore, the land of Israel is not abundant with natural resources as is Iraq, nor is it a commerce hub such as Syria, which may cause a higher demand and competitiveness for the land of Assyria. However, Israel's land is also in demand because of Zionism.

---

[309] Edward Said. Orientalism. P. 12

Christian Zionism, which supports the Jewish colonization of Palestine, commenced around the 19th century following the Protestant Reformation. Christian Zionism is a force among "powerful elites in England and United States." The Balfour Doctrine of England in 1917 "supported a national Jewish state in Palestine." In America, "Christian Zionism transcended into the United States" through Woodrow Wilson, Harry Truman, and Franklin Roosevelt because "all three administrations favored Zionism through beliefs realized from literal commands of biblical prophecies."[310] Through government funding of Israel, the United States and Britain helped established Israel as one of the largest military forces in the region. Consequently, Israel became a "military off-shoot for the United States and Britain, providing Israel with additional pre- positioned ammunition, weapons, and exchange of raw-data intelligence."[311]   With all these facts considered, Israel has an abundance of resources because of Zionism, which is the major difference between the Assyrians and Israelis. The Assyrians are enduring a resource dilemma, while Jewish organizations are more punctual than any Assyrian political organization seeking the same result Israel has achieved.

In 1929, Israel created the Jewish Agency, the primary organization responsible for the immigration ("Aliyah") and absorption of Jews and their families from the diaspora into Israel.[312] Since 1948, the Jewish Agency for Israel has been responsible for bringing 3 million immigrants to Israel[313] and offers transitional housing in "absorption centers" throughout the country.[314] The Jewish Agency played a central role in the founding and the building of the State of Israel, including the establishment of about 1000 towns and villages, and it continues to serve as the main link between Israel and Jewish communities around the world.[315] Its mission is to "inspire Jews throughout the world to connect with their people, heritages, and land,

---

[310] Noam Chomsky. Why does the U.S. support Israel? Interview. YouTube. 2016
[311] Noam Chomsky. Who Rules the World? Metropolitan Books. New York. 2016
[312] Jewish Agency: Aliyah. Jewish Agency. Retrieved March 12, 2015.
[313] Jewish Agency: About Us. Retrieved March 12, 2015
[314] Jewish Agency: Aliyah of Rescue. Jewish Agency. Retrieved March 12, 2015.
[315] Ibid.

and empower them to build a thriving Jewish future and a strong Israel."[316]   The organization's total operating budget in 2013 was $355,833,000, and its projected operating budget for 2014 is $369,206,000.[317]

Furthermore, the Israel lobby has been effective with systematic and continuous influence among legislators throughout the world. In particular, Israel's foreign aid received from the United States is extraordinary. To date, economic and military assistance to Israel has amounted to nearly $154 billion, the bulk of it compromising direct grants; Israel now receives on average about $3 billion in direct foreign assistance, an amount equal to 2 percent of Israel's Gross Domestic Product.[318]   Obviously, this type of support stems from lobbying groups and Jewish politicians in America and is the difference between the Assyrian political organizations and the Jewish organizations. Therefore, the process of democratization of the Israeli people in the Middle East may be a precedent and analogous case study for Assyrians to examine cautiously. In reality, Assyrian leadership reflects Palestinian leadership.

Three significant areas reveal the flaws impeding Palestinian political leadership that are parallel to current Assyrian leadership. The first is the struggle for legitimacy. The last elections of any sort took place in 2005–2006, and overdue local elections have been indefinitely postponed. The Palestine Liberation Organization (PLO) remains a potential vehicle for democratic decision- making, but serious reform is not on the horizon.[319]

The second critical problem is a lack of "creativity and strategic thinking when it comes to tactics. This has a number of root causes, the main point is a marked inability to adapt to circumstances with regard to the kind of smart resistance most appropriate for confronting

---

[316] Jewish Agency Annual Report 2014. Jewish Agency. Retrieved March 12, 2015.
[317] Ibid.
[318] John Mearsheimer. The Israel Lobby and US Foreign Policy. Farrah, Straus Gioux, New York 2008.
[319] Ben White. "The Problem with Palestinian Political Leadership." The Guardian, September 1, 2011.

colonization." Fear of losing control over the course of events can be one factor "inhibiting openness to change, which permits Israeli settlements and economy to increase independence from Palestinians."

The third problem is focus on power for its own sake rather than for the achievement of a specific goal. This criticism applies to both Fatah and Hamas, though the former has been guilty of it for a longer period of time and with more devastating consequences. Over the past five years or so, the conflict between these two factions has frequently resembled a fight over who can occupy the Bantustan palace—rather than who can serve most effectively the unfinished Palestinian revolution. The growing expressions of "dissatisfaction" particularly from young Palestinians, have "contributed to a hardening grip on power by two regimes that fear they stand to lose from an overhauled democratic system." Therefore, the Palestinian leadership is a "hollowed box"[320] with no legitimacy that parallels to any Assyrian secular organizations.

---

[320] Rashid Khalidi. "Palestine Now." Interview by Ahmed Shihab - Eldin. Vice News. HBO. March 25, 2016.

CHAPTER FIFTEEN– BECKONING ASPIRATIONS, ASSYRIA

The Assyrian community has endured the somber consistency of their times past. The effects of survival have led to most of the population being complacent in Western democracies and apathetic toward Assyrian social mobility. Although the pleasures of comfort are appropriate for many Assyrians, this complacency is not beneficial to Assyrian progression because it is counterproductive toward motivating reasonable nationalistic ideals around the global community. Thus, Assyrians must be motivated by common factors of human needs to help alleviate the effects of past persecution. These factors may induce a uniform authority that will enhance the opportunity of Assyrian progression.

In 1942, Abraham Maslow wrote "A Theory of Human Motivation," which analyzes the hierarchy of human needs and why those needs are timeless and indispensable. These theories are broken up into five segments and are divided based on their significance to human needs, with the most fundamental levels at the bottom and most imperative at the top.[321] Maslow set up a hierarchic theory of needs. Humans start with a weak disposition that is then fashioned fully as the person grows. If the environment is right, people will grow socially, actualizing the potentials they have inherited. If the environment is not right, which it is not for most Assyrians, they will not grow socially.

---

[321] A.H. Maslow. A Theory of Motivation. 1943. Psychological Review.

Maslow's hierarchy of five levels of basic needs include understanding, esthetic appreciation, and purely spiritual needs.[322] In the levels of the five basic needs, the person does not feel the second need until the demands of the first have been satisfied, nor the third until the second has been satisfied, and so on.[323] If Assyrians yearn to obliterate the resource dilemma, the Assyrian global population must collectively act upon each factor as motivating Assyrian development, specifically concentrating on the factors that tailor to collective communal growth rather than individualistic ambition.

Maslow's bottom factor of human motivation utilizes physiology.[324] Physiological factors included the need for food, shelter, sex, and sleep. Except for the Middle East, nearly all of the Assyrian population has food, shelter, rest, and intimate relationships. Despite the chaos and uncertainty in the Middle East, Assyrians may accomplish physiological factors. However, the fact that Assyrians in their indigenous homelands are struggling to obtain these basic rights should induce the Assyrian global population to overtly act upon ending this paucity of the Assyrian condition in the Middle East.

The second factor is safety and security. Safety and security are universal concerns. However, the potential for risk increases in countries with weak central governments. Therefore, the Assyrians in the Middle East, more than ever in war-torn Syria and overwhelmed Iraq- are in danger because of lack of safety and security. This lack of safety and security for Assyrians has induced recent military mobilization in the area. However, those Assyrians in the diaspora can address safety and security more resourcefully through political integration coupled with democratic and transparent cooperation.

---

[322] W. Mittleman. Maslow's Study of Self-Actualization: A Reinterpretation. 1990. Journal of Humanistic Psychology
[323] Ibid.
[324] Ibid.

The third factor is belongingness and love. These factors generate from interpersonal connection and the human need to be accepted by a group with others. This factor is approachable for the Assyrian community because the community is small and situated in enclaves in their respective adopted home countries. Further, as previously noted, generational parallels exist between Assyrian age groups, which link a sense of self-sufficient, survival, and revival of Assyrian nationalism. Additionally, social media and volunteer tourism may converge the sense of belongingness within a dispersed Assyrian population. However, for the Middle Eastern Assyrians, there must be a peace of mind of liberty and dignity and the ability to accomplish a sense of perpetual love without being constrained by fear.

The fourth factor generates from self-esteem that is created through a human need to feel respected. This factor may be achieved through profession or hobby individually. While some Assyrians have generated esteem for themselves, many Assyrians living in foreign surroundings may have diminished self-esteem caused by a lack of contribution or value to society. Low self- esteem or an inferiority complex may result from imbalances during this level in the hierarchy. People with low self-esteem often need respect from others; they may feel the need to seek fame or glory. However, fame or glory will not help the person to build his or her self-esteem until that person accepts who they are internally. Psychological imbalances such as depression can hinder the person from obtaining a higher level of self-esteem or self-respect. Therefore, it is essential for each Assyrian to motivate every other with genuine and sincere feelings of self-importance regardless of the level of societal value or contribution.

Maslow's final factor is self-actualization and self-transcendence, which is an individual realizing one's full potential and overtly acting upon the potential to achieve an objective. In other words, to understand ones worth and to diligently and competently attempt to become what one actually is through selflessness and spirituality. These five factors describe the pattern that human motivations generally move through. Therefore, most of the factors listed above may draw a nationalistic realization that reformation of allocating resources must be completed in order to achieve the fulfillments of the hierarchy of human needs. Once the reformation has been implemented, then Assyria will gain positive force to proceed to an Assyrian nation-state.

Historically, Assyrian culture has obsessed with its accomplishments, virtues, self-sufficiency, and tradition. But it is important to understand what motivates a human to proceed to accomplish certain objectives and goals. The Assyrian global community must use Maslow's factors to induce motivation toward organization and social mobility, which are prerequisites for a formalization of development.

When Assyrians gain momentum and attempt to formalize development, there is no doubt that a unconstructive response will arise because of the complex web of external and internal interests in the Middle East. A large Kurdish population has grown in northern Iraq for the past two decades, so it would be a benefit to the Assyrians to practice diplomacy with the Kurdish people.

The Kurdish population ranges from 20–35 million people worldwide. The Kurdish population in Iraq is around 6–6.5 million, which constitutes 17 percent of Iraq's population; in Syria, the Kurdish population is around 2–3 million and constitutes 11 percent of the population.[325] Many Kurds seek outright political autonomy for the Kurdish inhabited areas of Syria, similar to Iraqi Kurdistan in Iraq, or independence as part of Kurdistan. Although the obvious conflict between land rights is evident concerning the Assyrian and Kurdish relationships, the region will never fulfill its quest for peace without both groups cordially working together. The Kurdish population substantially outnumbers the Assyrian population; therefore, it would be in the Kurdish population's best interest to demonstrate democratic ideals by concurrently governing the regions. Furthermore, the Assyrians are the indigenous people of the region and Kurdish powers would presumably not be obliged to govern with discriminatory impact that may cause conflict.

Persuading a majority of the Assyrian global population to share land with the Kurdish population may be difficult; however, one must understand that modality of nationalism may be modified to prevent hazardous sentiment. The same "we're all in it together" attitude that elicits mutual sacrifice within a nation can easily degenerate into jingoistic contempt for all things foreign. Indeed, the "two emotions tend to reinforce one another."[326] Examples include Britain employing virtue and solidarity as when it fought Nazi Germany. America's cold war with the Soviet Union inspired and provided justification for billions of dollars of public expenditure on highways, education, and research. However, history offers ample warnings of how "zero sum" nationalism— the assumption that either we win or they win—can "corrode public values to the point at which citizens support policies that marginally improve their own welfare while harming everyone else on the planet, thus forcing other nations to do the same in defense."[327]

---

325 CIA Fact book. Kurdish Population. Retrieved March 12, 2015.
326 Work of Nations. P. 305
327 Work of Nations. P. 306

The same "social discipline and fierce loyalty that have elicited sacrifices among a group of people have also, in this century, generated mind-numbing atrocities."[328] Unbridled nationalism can cause civic values to degenerate personally. As well "Individuals to grow paranoid about foreign agents in their midst; civil liberties are restricted on grounds of national interest. Neighbors begin to distrust on another, causing tribal allegiances that can tear nations apart."[329]

An example of "zero sum" nationalism in the Assyrian community includes the conflict between agents allocating resources for Assyrians in Iraq's Iraqi Kurdistan Parliament. The Assyrian Democratic Movement, Zowaa, is conflicted with former Assyrian politician, Sargis Aghajan Mamendo (Aghajan) and the political party Aghajan organized called the United Front Popular council.[330]

Aghajan participated in the Kurdish regional parliament in provinces of Iraqi Kurdistan. He was appointed finance minister for Iraqi Kurdistan on May 7, 2006, and is in close relationship with Nechirvan Idris Barzani, the prime minster of the Kurdish Regional Government of Northern Iraq. Aghajan's cooperation with Kurdish politicians has funded roads, settlement towns, and apartment homes for the Assyrian population. One specific project is in Bakhdida, an Assyrian city located 20 miles southeast of Mosul, where a construction of a large multipurpose hall for the Assyrian population has been undertaken. Furthermore, in August 2006, Aghajan was awarded as "Knight Commander of the Order of Saint Gregory the Great" by Pope Benedict XVI to honor his work with the Assyrian community

---

[328] Ibid.

[329] Work of Nations. P. 308

[330] According to Wikileaks Cable: 09BAGHDAD1785_a, According to Kanna ADM views its primary competition coming. . . from the "Ishtar" list, which is also known as the Chaldean Syriac Assyrian People's Council. According to Kanna, "the Ishtar list is not an independent party, but a Kurdish Democratic Party (KDP) creation that promises to represent the Christian community but will ultimately align with the KDP."

in Iraq. Aghajan was awarded the title, which is one of the highest and most widely recognized pontifical orders, for his contribution to the Assyrian community and his work for Christians in Iraq.[331]

Zowaa claims that the Kurdistan party is using the United Front to undermine Zowaa's ability, performance, and achievements within this region. Zowaa's argument states that KRG is being "used to beautify its own image in order to annex Assyrian settlements in the Nineveh Plains."[332] Further claims have even asserted that Aghajan is a "covert agent for the KRG and assembled his own militia, which is accused of harassing Assyrian candidates during the 2009 Nineveh province elections."[333] These claims may have no plausibility because no neutral fact finder confirms such claims with corroborating evidence except claims intended for political propaganda.[334]

---

[331] http://christianityinkurdistan.blogspot.com/2008/02/sarkis-aghajan-mamendu.html

[332] Assyria Council of Europe, Hammurabi Human Rights Organization. "The Struggle to Exist: An Introduction to the Assyrians and their Human Rights Situation in the New Iraq." AINA.org. P. 44. Retrieved 18 October 2011.

[333] According to Wikileaks Cable: 09BAGHDAD1785_a, "Kanna accused Ishtar of engaging in electoral fraud to win the seat reserved for Christians on the Baghdad Provincial Council in January 2009 and claimed that they were already engaging in voter intimidation in the Kurdistan region in order to influence the July 25 elections." Kanna argued that Ishtar will "probably win two-to-three seats if it is allowed to continue with its heavy-handed tactics."

[334] According to Wikileaks Cable: 09BAGHDAD612_a, Kanna claimed that Yezidis were "pressured by Kurds to vote for Kurdish parties." Without offering any evidence, Kanna opined "many polling stations had run out of ballots in the afternoon because the Kurds had bussed in Yezidis from outlying villages and had them vote for Kurdish lists, even if they were not listed in the voter rolls." Kanna recounted that, in Baghdad, "a Christian priest had been turned away from the polling station he had voted at in past elections because his name could not be found on the voter list." According to Wikileaks Cable: 09BAGHDAD612_a, Kanna offered no evidence that the Kurdish parties pressured Yezidi voters. "Our election observation teams found few such cases. In fact, the anti-KRG candidate beat the pro-KRG candidate in the election for the seat set aside to represent the Yezidi community, and more than half of the Kurdish Alliance's provincial councilors will be Yezidis." "In addition, the phenomenon of voters not finding their names on voters' lists was widespread on election day throughout Iraq, as were allegations that political parties around the country had provided buses to transport voters to polling sites."

Further, Zowaa's argument lacks credibility because the Kurdistan region is allocating resources for a minority group that needs adequate funds, a common practice in parliamentary and legislative political institutions, but Zowaa's lack of transparency and visceral opposition of sharing power has caused members to disassociate with the Assyrian Democratic Movement forming another political organization in 2013 called the Sons of Mesopotamia.[335] Contrarily, Aghajan's party failed to take the opportunity to create a political community by communicating, acknowledging and cooperating with the achievements Zowaa has performed. Without a real political community in which to learn, refine, and practice the ideals of justice and fairness, Zowaa and the Sons of Mesopotamia found these accomplishments to be meaningless abstractions. Therefore, Aghajan

---

[335] According to Wikileaks Cable: 09BAGHDAD1785_a, "The party's superior organization translated into immediate benefits during the CPA era, when MP Kanna was the sole Christian representative on the Iraqi Governing Council." Since that time, "the ADM's attempts to portray itself as speaking for the entire Christian community have irritated many within the larger Chaldean and Syriac bodies, which view themselves as not only numerically superior, but also distinct from the Assyrians." According to Wikileaks Cable: 09BAGHDAD1785_a, One Iraqi Christian leader, former Minister of Displacement and Migration Pascale Warda, herself a current ADM member, described Kanna as "singularly obsessed with being the sole voice of Iraq's Christian community and the ADM as being a one-man show, with him at the helm." PM Advisor Bakoos described how "in the run up to the Iraqi Constitutional Convention in 2005, the Christian community was asked to put forward a list of five persons to represent them." According to Bakoos, "Kanna insisted on providing his own list to the Convention, which was heavy on representatives from the ADM to the exclusion of other Christian political parties."

failed to help create a sense of solidarity and generosity.[336] Paranoia caused by "zero sum" nationalism is more volatile than helpful to Assyrian progression. Zowaa's focus on national well-being is dangerously narrow in relation to the biggest problem facing Assyrians—their resource dilemma. In addition, Zowaa's application of "zero sum" nationalism has deviated from its original message of democratic ideals and resenting old tribal conflicts, the motivation for the Sons of Mesopotamia to organize. Currently, several political parties fragment Assyrian representation in Northern Iraq; Zowaa, Aghajan's United Popular Council, the Sons of Mesopotamia, and others within the Iraqi Kurdistan Parliament. Presumably, the United Front, Zowaa, and the Sons of Mesopotamia could allocate resources from Kurdish funds and from Assyrian funds, then the pool of assets would be mutually exclusive for Assyrian development. However, the notion of "zero sum" nationalism has endangered the possible economic prosperity stemming from two resources. Aghajan was an Assyrian who was allocating resources for Assyrians in Iraq, and now Aghajan's focus on allocating resources for Assyrians has dissipated. Aghajan no longer funds the Christian community in Iraq and is no longer finance minister to the KRG. His Winter 2011 project was his last.[337] Further, the reduction of members in Zowaa will only exacerbate the scarce resources for futile political reasons. This is an example of "zero sum" nationalism inducing an Assyrian resource dilemma. Both parties must feel responsible for each other's causes

---

336 According to Wikileaks Cable: 09BAGHDAD1785_a, KRG Minister of Finance Sarkis Aghajan strongly advocated an autonomous zone, noting that "if Christians had been granted their own areas previously they would have been able to retain their lands and their communities instead of the mass emigration now underway (Reftel)." He noted others speak out "against an autonomous zone, but are motivated by personal conflicts instead of working to save Christians in Iraq." "A referendum must be held," Sarkis explained, as it would allow the Christian community to determine its fate in Iraq. Yonadem Kanna, Secretary General of the Assyrian Democratic Movement (ADM), on the other hand, advocated, "providing local administrative control to religious minority communities per Article 125 of the Iraqi Constitution in a meeting June 12, rather than an autonomous zone based in the Nineveh Plains as Sarkis urged." For example, Kanna said that parts of Baghdad could serve "as key areas in which to allocate increased local administrative control, with what he numbered to be 27,000 strong Christian families living in Baghdad."
337 Aghajan was officially replaced with Bayiz Saeed Mohammad. Aghajan was the KRG finance minister until October 2008.

because both share a common history, participate in common cultures, and possibly face a common fate. Assyrians must examine the virtues of cooperation with the KRG, thus reducing the resource dilemma felt by many vulnerable Assyrians. No longer should aid from KRG be perceived to be "taking over" Assyria; instead, the funding from KRG and Aghajan is more accurately perceived as helping Assyrians to become more productive around the Nineveh Plains.

Whether the Kurdish populations are in control of northern Iraq will always be questioned with an Assyrian presence there, regardless of whether the KRG is added to their operations. Assyria is not losing land because of the KRG but gaining resources to help reclaim the land within the Middle East. The KRG is heavily enthusiastic about a positive reflective view from global powers toward its region. Therefore, the appointment of Aghajan may have been a valuable insight into how to acquire resources from funds outside the Assyrian community.

By acquiring funds from the KRG, the Assyrians living in Iraq have received adequate resources. And these funds have no intention or suitability of being misappropriated because the funds are allocated within the region. Therefore, the funds are intended to remain in northern Iraq and help improve the standard of living for the Assyrian community. Therefore, the zero-sum nationalism of "us or them" may be hindering Assyrian progression when a share of KRG profits might be more favorable to the Assyrian cause than hindering.

Despite enthusiasm, major problems regarding the KRG's structure and system preclude elements of a democratic society. These problems include political factions involving the military and institutions, lack of resources, no constitutional authority, and corruption. Thus, all create a system of discrimination toward the Assyrian indigenous population. According to Human Rights Watch, "KRG authorities have relied on intimidation, threats, and arbitrary arrests and detentions, more than actual violence, in their efforts to secure support of minority communities for their agenda regarding the disputed territories"[338] A representative of the Assyrian community described Kurdish treatment of Assyrians as "the overarching, omnipresent reach of a highly effective and authoritarian regime that has much of the population under control through fear."[339]

Political Factions

"The wide array of Kurdish political parties and groups reflects the internal divisions among the Kurds", which often follow "tribal, linguistic, and national fault lines in addition to political disagreements and rivalries."[340] Tensions have mounted among the two dominant Iraqi Kurdish political parties—the Kurdistan Democratic Party (KDP) and Patriotic Union of Kurdistan (PUK)—and a third reform party named Gorran.

---

[338] Samir Muscati and Peter Bouckaert, On Vulnerable Ground. Human Rights Watch. November 10 2009.
[339] Ibid.
[340] "The Time of the Kurds," Council on Foreign Relations, July 29, 2015, www.cfr.org/middle-east-and-north-africa/time-kurds/p36547

The problem is a polarized society as a result of the internal conflicts, causing a lot of mistrust and a lot of rumors and misperceptions. "We are dealing with perception more than with reality."[341] "PUK and KDP are afraid of each other. There is no trust between them. The only thing to make it better, even if slowly, is to increase trust in the elections."[342]

"The biggest problem of the military, everything else aside, is that it is bipartisan; it is politicized. This is because they both originated from revolutionary means. Then there is the civil war." There is complete distrust: "Another problem is that in all of Iraq people never understood the military as a means for defense outside but always as a means toward the own people, to calm the population, to break protests, to kill the opposition."[343]

Assyrian political parties such as the Assyrian Democratic Movement, Sons of Mesopotamia, and the Bet-Nahrain/Ishtar party remain deadlocked because of a hegemony struggle.

Lack of Resources

At the moment, the region seems to be following the same path as other rentier states: high dependency on oil revenues, an increasingly bloated government sector, requiring subsidizing services, an imported food supply, and constant step backs on democratization.[344] Ever-increasing student graduates need to be provided jobs, benefits, and services. If any of these payments stops or decreases, there could be a risk of social instability.[345]

---

[341] Verena, Gruber. Revisiting Civil-Military-Relations Theory - The Case of the Kurdish Regional Government of Iraq. Master's thesis, Lund University, 2015. Lund, Sweden: Verena Gruber, 2015.
[342] Mohammad, Yusuf. Interviewed by Verena Gruber. Qualitative Interview. Erbil, 04/09/14.
[343] Chia Mustafah, Nashirwan. Interviewed by Verena Gruber. Qualitative Interview. Sulaymaniyah, 10/11/14.
[344] Denise Natali. "Kurdistan seems to be following a reinter state." The Kurdish Tribune. December 21, 2013.
[345] Ibid.

The other problem is that the KRG does not have the quantity of resources or level of revenues available in Gulf states and, because of its landlocked status, will be dependent on different states for its economic survival. Supplemental assistance is scarce. In regards to the budgeting process, the KRG did not receive anything from the Iraqi side for eight years.[346] "Further, defense funding is inadequate and speculative because "now we pay the Peshmerga by cutting off budget every month from all other ministries because the Peshmerga do not have a budget. They are supposed to receive this money from the Iraqi defense system."[347]

---

[346] Jafar Sheikah Mustafah. Interviewed by Verena Gruber. Qualitative Interview. Qaradigh, 26/09/14.
[347] Hermin, Hawrami. Interviewed by Verena Gruber. Qualitative Interview. Erbil, 01/12/14.

Lack of Constitutional Authority

The KRG structure has been hindered due to lack of constitutional authority and cohesion within the KRG, its political parties, and Peshmerga military unit. "The biggest problem we encounter is that people think that this is the only way of administering a country. People who lived here their entire life are after loyalty."[348] "...Having a unified force in Kurdistan is somehow difficult. Right now we do not have a constitution. If you do not have a constitution how you could establish an institution, let alone a unified military institution?"[349]

Corruption

In the KRG regions, corruption has caused "inequality in the government, favoritism, the bad in the ministries, the relationship to Baghdad, tribalism of KDP, family structure of PUK, Peshmerga wages, transparency" ... We also explained to them what [terms] mean, for example what is a budget. People did not know."[350] The problem is deemed systemic. "It is not just about changing an individual minister; like in Kafka, there is a system that is a nightmare and forces you to resort to favoritism."[351]

---

[348] Resool, Sheroosh (Haji). Interviewed by Verena Gruber. Qualitative Interview. Sulaymaniyah, 10/11/14.
[349] Sahil, Ali. Interviewed by Verena Gruber. Qualitative Interview. Makhmour, 17/11/14.
[350] Dracy, Babhkhar. Interviewed Verena Gruber. Qualitative Interview. Sulaymaniyah, 10/11/14.
[351] Omar, Hoshyar. Interviewed by Verena Gruber. Qualitative Interview. Sulaymaniyah, 13/11/14.

One obstacle for institutionalization is oil; there is too much money outside the government. Also, the judiciary system is biased towards the parties and corruption is a big test."[352] Corruption creates economic challenge faced by the Christian IDP community. A construction engineer from Basra named Laith Alqa, commented that he "refused to reopen his construction business, despite considerable potential contract work, due to the amount of bribes and kickbacks he would have to pay. KRG is the corruption affecting activity in the private sector."[353]

Exxon

Iraq, while under the rule of Prime Minister Nouri al-Maliki was moving toward "dictatorship and civil war." Former Prime Minister al-Maliki stated, "we will see a rise in violence and a total paralysis in Baghdad," he recalled saying. Iraq was likely to align itself more closely with Iran, which will "have an adverse impact on U.S. companies." Iraqi conflict induced Exxon executives to focus on Northern Iraq. Because they had signed a $25 billion deal with Iraq to develop West Qurna, one of the largest oil fields in the country, other contractual agreements with the KRG were assented to and Exxon proceeded to expand their desire for profits.[354]

---

[352] Ahmed, Muhammad Ali. Interviewed by Verena Gruber. Qualitative Interview. Sulaymaniyah, 10/11/14.

[353] Al-Sahab. "Irq-Iraq-Middle-East." Wikileaks cable: GI Files 821824.

[354] Dmitry, Coles, Isabel Zhdannikov, and Ned Parker. "Special Report: How Exxon helped make Iraqi Kurdistan." Reuters. December 03, 2014. Accessed April 13, 2016. http://www.reuters.com/article/us-mideast-crisis-kurdistan-specialrepor-idUSKCN0JH18720141204.

Because Iraq is "socially thin" [lacking basic infrastructure and social services diminished by war and postwar deconstruction], Exxon induced the KRG to push for Kurdistan to become a separate "petrol state," similar to "Angola, Chad, and Nigeria."[355] Thus Exxon's goal is to circumvent legal accountability and reduce northern Iraq's authority to " the ability to provide contractual legal authority that can legitimate the extraction work of transitional firms "[356] Similarly as in Chad, Nigeria and Angola, a third of the profits from excavations will be accumulated by Exxon and rerouted to Anglo or European banks for development elsewhere, leaving Northern Iraq's sovereignty diminished.

The six regions Exxon won were scattered around the autonomous region. One area was near Turkey and another near the border with Iran. The three most controversial regions of oil exploration were along the line that divides Kurdistan and the rest of Iraq, straddling areas whose control is disputed between Arbil and Baghdad.[357]

The Kurds included the blocks in the deal and later managed to bring the governor of Nineveh, one of the provinces affected, on board. Exxon's desire for profits is evident from their controversial dealings with autocratic governments and speaking out against United States sanctions on petroleum rich countries.[358]

---

[355] Trisha, Khale Tyrannosaurus Rex. Jacobin, (No.26), 25-31. August, 2017
[356] Ibid.
[357] Dmitry, Coles, Isabel Zhdannikov, and Ned Parker. "Special Report: How Exxon helped make Iraqi Kurdistan." Reuters. December 03, 2014
[358] Ibid.

For Assyrians, the "tightly woven tapestry of oppression, dispossession, and repression"[359] represent the future for Assyrians in their indigenous homeland, which is now controlled by transnational corporations and a non-Assyrian community that "prioritizes pumping oil out of the ground inexpensively while ignoring the indigenous population."[360] Further, Exxon will have no interest in developing Iraq for citizens but rather exploit the resources for its own profits that encroach on Assyrian land, exacerbating wealth inequality and depreciating and destroying Assyrian indigenous land.

Kurdish Referendum

On June 7, 2017, Masoud Barzani, the leader of the Kurdish independence referendum announced that the Kurdish community in Iraq would proceed with a plan for Kurdish autonomy from the Iraqi national government. Independence for Kurds is a gain for the Kurdish community but a loss for the Assyrian Iraqi community. The process to Kurdish independence has included illegal land grabs, local government coups, and discrimination against Assyrians, which places the Assyrians in a familiar quandary of political factions caused by colonialism, thus resulting in a lack of resources to mobilize adequate resistance and progress. Despite divide between Kurdish political parties, the Kurdish community continues to push for independence causing tension and assault among the Assyrian population.

Although the referendum failed because of power displayed from Baghdad, the election serves as a precursor that the conflict between Kurds and Baghdad will leave Assyrians vulnerable to incidental and collateral damages. It is reasonable to anticipate further attempts at land grabs, ousting of elected local Assyrian officials, discrimination and oppression.

---

[359] Trish, Khale. "Tyrannosaurus Rex." Jacobin, (No.26) 25. August, 2017
[360] Ibid.

Philosopher of Sociology Michael Ignatieff expressed, "We think of ourselves not as human beings first, but as sons, and daughters ... tribesmen and neighbors. It is this dense web of relations and the meanings which they give to life which satisfies the needs which really matter to us."[361] In the web of relations in the Middle East, the Assyrians must present a unified front to work with the KRG to solve the resource dilemma. Such an ambition should not be regarded as a threat to the well-being and security of Assyrians. On the contrary, these efforts add to the total wealth of Assyrians around the world. Assyrian political organizations should pursue the same worthy goal. However, political organizations have created an awkward and limited means of achieving resources, thus limiting the total wealth of Assyrians.

If Assyrians seek to govern their own progress, they must solve the territorial dispute with the Kurdish population. The ability to govern in the Middle East during a territorial dispute is an incontrovertible characteristic of an effective Middle Eastern State. However, Assyrians must also reflect upon their process of democratization within the scope of democratic principles to avoid the atrocities that are caused by zero-sum nationalism.

---

[361] Michael Ignatieff, The Needs of Strangers (New York: Viking Penguin, 1985), P.29

CHAPTER SIXTEEN– CONCLUSION

The Assyrian people have endured a thoroughness of persecution and neglect throughout their existence. After their empire was dissipated, the common trend of the Assyrian standard of living was persecution, mass migration, genocide, and under-inclusive representation. This trend has been a timeless recurrence for generations of Assyrians. The invasion of Iraq and the civil war in Syria are now conflicts that further Assyrian oppression. Furthermore, the Assyrians have endured being spread across the four corners of the Earth.

Although the Assyrian culture has been soundly resilient and has maintained its identity through mostly religious institutions, there now must be a clear authority on how to conform the idea of Assyria into an actual process. Assyrians should embrace its culture and language. Individual Assyrians may further their awareness of Assyrian progression by expanding their bearings and being confident about new ideas and beliefs. In order to achieve that understanding, there must be a national bargain between all Assyrians living in the diaspora, coupled with political integration and international cooperation of every Assyrian organization.

Assyrians share more than humanity with each other; they share a responsibility toward one another to form a particular bond to elicit sacrifice toward the nation because external and internal factors have given some individual Assyrians a highly specialized education to maintain an appropriate life perspective on the world's problems and possibilities. Disregarding those with a strong patriotic impulse, the millennial Assyrian is likely to resist zero-sum nationalistic solutions because globalization has caused individuals to behave more responsibly toward their personal gain. It is vital that this lifestyle does not engender resignation. Even the highly specialized, educated Assyrian is sensitive to the problems that plague the world, and these dilemmas may seem so "intractable and overpowering in their global dimensions that any attempt to remedy them appears futile."[362]

"The greatest enemy of progress is a sense of hopelessness; from a vantage point that takes in the full enormity of the world's ills, real progress may seem beyond reach."[363] Within smaller political units like towns, cities, states, and even nations, problems may seem solvable; even a tiny improvement can seem large on this smaller scale. As a result, where the "nationalist is apt to feel that a sacrifice is both valorous and potentially effective, the cosmopolitan may be overcome by its apparent uselessness."[364]

It should not come as a surprise, then, that all great social reform movements have begun locally. Particularly for Assyrians, the Code of Hammurabi, the Assyrian Church of the East, political organizations and politicians, were all ignited locally and expanded in scope subsequently. Focus, patience, and devotion are essential factors in expanding the scope of democratic ideals. Therefore, those who aim to reform Assyrian progress in one "great swoop often have difficulty signing up credulous recruits."[365]

---

[362] Work of Nations. P. 310
[363] Ibid.
[364] Jonathan Glover, "It Makes No Difference Whether or Not I Do It," Supplemental Proceedings of the Aristotelian Society, New York, 1975.
[365] Work of Nations. P. 314

In short, while a specialized educated Assyrian provides useful and appropriate perspectives on many of the world's problems and avoids the pitfalls of ignorance, it may discourage the very steps necessary to remedy the problems it illuminates. However, ineffective in the face of the Assyrian resource dilemma is a bunch of foolish nationalists intent on making their particular organization number one. Therefore, there must be a balanced Assyrian leadership reflecting the Assyrian community rather than indifferent cosmopolitans and headstrong nationalists.

BIBLIOGRAPHY

"ACERO | Assyrian Church of the East Relief Organization." ACERO. Web. 13 Mar. 2015.

Allison, S. T., Beggan, J. K., & Midgley, E. H. (1996). The quest for "similar instances" and "simultaneous possibilities" Metaphors in social dilemma research. Journal of Personality and Social Psychology, 71, 979-497.

Ágoston and Alan Masters, Gábor and Bruce (2009). Encyclopedia of the Ottoman Empire. Infobase Publishing. p. 583.

Allam, Hannah. "Records show how Iraqi extremists withstood US anti-terror efforts." McClatchy News. 25 June 2014.

"Anbar Picture Grows Clearer, and Bleaker." The Washington Post 28 Nov. 2006. Web. 8 Mar. 2015.

Asia News 2010, 'Mosul, a Christian businessman killed as the faithful celebrate their new archbishop,' 18 January 2011.

Associated Press. Iraqi Constitution. Washington Post. October 2005.

Associated Press. Bishru Juil. Atour Magazine. January 2011.

Assyrian International News Agency. 'Assyrians in Tehran Demonstrate Against Baghdad Church Massacre,' 17 November 2010.

Assyria Council of Europe, 'Ethnic discrimination in the Iraqi police force: The case of Assyrians in the Nineveh Plain of northern Iraq,' December 2010.

Baum, Wilhelm Baum; Dietmar W. Winkler (2003). The Church of the East: A Concise History. Routledge. pp. 150–155. September 22, 2010.

Benedict, Ruth. The chrysanthemum and the sword: Patterns of Japanese culture. Pp. 233-239. Columbia University Press. New York. 1989

Benjamin Braude und Bernard Lewis (ed.), Christians and Jews in the Ottoman Empire. The

Functioning of a Plural Society, 2 vol., New York and London 1982.

Bendix, Reinhard. Max Weber, an Intellectual Portrait. Berkeley: University of California, 1977. Print.

Biography of His Holiness, The Assyrian Martyr, The Late Mar Eshai Shimun XXIII". Committee of the 50th Anniversary of the Patriarchate of Mar Eshai Shimun XXIII. Retrieved 23 September 2011.

Bolingbroke's Works. Six Letters, Addressed to His Excellency Earl Fitzwilliam ... By Bolingbroke. Vol. 1. London: Printed by T. Davies, 1775. Print.

Bowen, Jeremy. Six Days: How the 1967 War Shaped the Middle East. London: Simon & Schuster. 2003.

Bowles, Samuel and Herbert Gintis. A Cooperative Species. Human Reciprocity and Its Evolution. Princeton University Press. Princeton NJ. 2013

Brownstein, Scott. "Self-funded & Deep Rooted. How ISIS Makes Millions." CNN. Cable News Network, 7 Oct. 2014. Web. 10 Mar. 2015.

Bruenig, Matt. Wealth Inequality Is Higher Than Ever. Retrieved from https://www.jacobinmag.com/2017/10/wealth-inequality-united-states-federal-reserve. October 1, 2017

Burke, Edmund. Reflections on the Revolution in France. Vol. 2. New York: Penguin, 1968. 221. Print.

C. H. W. Johns (1904). Babylonian and Assyrian laws, contracts, and letters. Kessinger Publishing.

Caris, Charles, and Samuel Reynolds. "ISIS Governance in Syria." Institute for the Study of War Syria Updates. 1 July 2014. Web. 1 Mar. 2015.

Chandrasekaran, Rajiv. Imperial Life in the Emerald City: Inside Iraq's Green Zone. FOOTNOTE: World Bank, World Development Report 1990 (Oxford World Bank, 1990), 178- 79; New Mexico coalition for literacy, New Mexico Literacy Profile, 2005-2006 Programs, www.nmcl.org.

Childress, Sarah, Evan Wexler, and Chris Amico. "Who Runs the Islamic State?" PBS. PBS, 28 Oct. 2014. Web. 1 Mar. 2015.

Chibber, Vivek. The Twentieth Century Left Socialists Plenty of Lessons. Will We Heed them? Jacobin.

Chomsky, Noam. Requiem for the American dream. Seven Stories Press. New York. 2016

Chomsky, Noam. Who Rules the World? Metropolitan Books. New York. 2016

Chulov, Michael. "How an Arrest in Iraq Revealed Isis's $2bn Jihadist Network." The

Guardian. 15 June 2014. Web. 17 June 2014.

"CPA Order Number 1." Dissolution of Entities Iraq Coalition. 1 June 2003. Web. 3 Mar. 2015.

"CPA Order Number 2." Dissolution of Entities Iraq Coalition. 1 June 2003. Web. 3 Mar. 2015.

Coalition Provisional Authority, Order Number 37 Tax Strategy for 2003, September 19, 2003, www.iraqcoalition.org; Coalition Provisional Authority, Order Number 39 Foreign Investment, December 20, 2003, www.iraqcoalition.org;

Dadesho, Sargon. The Assyrian National Question. Bet-Nahrain Press. 1988

Dahl, Robert. What is Politics: Modern Political Analysis. Prentice Hall Publishers. 1963 P. 54

Deputy Secretary Wolfowitz Interview with Sam Tannenhaus," Vanity Fair, News Transcript, May 9, 2003, www.defenselink.mil.

Definition of Dilemma. Dictionary.com. Web. 1 Mar. 2014.

Definition of Resource. Dictionary.com. Web. 1 Mar. 2014.

Dickens, Mark "The Church of the East" The American Foundation for Syriac Studies. October 2012.

Di Giovanni, Janine, Leah McGrath-Goodwin, and Damien Sharkov. "How Does ISIS Fund Its Reign of Terror?" Newsweek 6 Nov. 2014. Print.

"Ethnic Cleansing on a Historical Scale." Amnesty International. 2 Sept. 2014. Web. 1 Mar. 2015.

Fisher, Max. "How ISIS Is Exploiting the Economics of Syria's Civil War." Vox. 12 June 2014. Web. 17 June 2014.

FOOTNOTE: 2007 Index of Economic Freedom (Washington, DC: Heritage Foundation and The Wall Street Journal, 2007), 326, www.heritage.org.

Friedman, L. Thomas. "What Were They Thinking?" New York Times, October 7, 2005.

Gaunt, David "The Assyrian Genocide of 1915," Assyrian Genocide Research Center, 2009.

Gigerenzer, Gerd. How to Make Cognitive Delusions Disappear: "Beyond Heuristic Biases. Oxford: European Review of Social Psychology, 1991. 83-115. Print.

Glover, Jonathan. It Makes No Difference Whether or Not I Do It, "Supplemental Proceedings of the Aristotelian Society" New York, 1975. 29. Print.

"Gunmen in Iraq's Ramadi Announce Sunni Emirate." Reuters. Thomson Reuters, 18 Oct. 2006. Web. 15 Dec. 2014.

Healy, Mark (1991). The Ancient Assyrians. London: Osprey. 1991.

Hoffman, Meredith. "Islamic State Releases Small Group after Mass Kidnapping." VICE News. 1 Mar. 2015. Web. 1 Mar. 2015.

Husry, K (April 1974), "The Assyrian Affair of 1933 (I)", International Journal of Middle East Studies (Cambridge University Press) 5 (3): 161–176.

Ignatieff, Michael. The Needs of Strangers. New York, N.Y., U.S.A.: Viking, 1985. Print.

Imber, Colin (2002). The Ottoman Empire, 1300–1650: The Structure of Power. Palgrave Macmillan. p. 53.

Interview, Suzan Younan. Gishru July19, 2013.
Interview, Suzan Younan. Gishru, July18, 2013.

IOM, 'IOM Emergency needs assessments – Displacement of Christians to the North of Iraq,' January 2011.

Iraq Democracy Project. Policy Briefing. October 13, 2008. "Iraq Government to Pay Sunni Groups." US & Canada. Al Jazeera, 3 Oct. 2008. Web. 8 Mar. 2014.

"Iraqi Christian Church Burnings Confirmed by EU Delegations." Iraq News, the Latest Iraq News. Web. 10 Mar. 2015.

"ISIL & Al Qaeda." Washington Institute for Near East Policy 1 June 2014. Web. 3 Mar. 2015.

"Islamic State Says Women in Mosul Must Wear Full Veil or Be Punished." Irish Times. 26 July 2014. Web. 1 Mar. 2015.

"ISIS Is Actively Recruiting Female Fighters to Brutalize Other Woman." Business Insider. Business Insider, Inc. Web. 1 Mar. 2015.

"James Baker's Double Life"; World Bank, "Data Sheet for Iraq," October 23, 2006, www.worldbank.org.

Jenkins, Phillip "The Lost History of Christianity: The Thousand-Year Golden Age of the Church in the Middle East, Africa, and Asia — and How It Died (San Francisco: Harper One, 2008).

Joel, Elias. "The Genetics of Modern Assyrians and Their Relationship to Other People of the Middle East" University of California School of Medicine, San Francisco. July 2000.

"Jordan Carries out Air Strikes in Iraq Killing 55 IS Militants." I24news. 4 Feb. 2015. Web. 4 Feb. 2015.

Judea, Pearl Heuristics: Intelligent Search Strategies for Computer Problem Solving. New York, Addison-Wesley, p. vii. 1983

Kaplow, Larry. "Attacked Again." Newsweek 13 June 2007. Web. 15 June 2007.

Khale, Trisha. Tyrannosaurus Rex. Jacobin, (No.26), 25-31. August, 2017

Khalidi, Rashid. "Palestine Now." Interview by Ahmed Shihab - Eldin. Vice News. HBO. March 25, 2016.

Khosoreva, Anahit. "The Assyrian Genocide in the Ottoman Empire and Adjacent Territories" in The Armenian Genocide: Cultural and Ethical Legacies. Ed. Richard G. Hovannisian. New Brunswick, NJ: Transaction Publishers, 2007.

Klein, Naomi, The Shock Doctrine: The Rise of Disaster Capitalism, 327. New York, NY: Penguin, 2007.

Knickmeyer, Ellen. "Bombing Shatters Mosque in Iraq." The Washington Post 23 Feb. 2006. Web. 11 Feb. 2011.

Kornbluth, Jacob. Inequality for all. DVD. 2013.

Lalani, Muntaz, 'Still Targeted: Continued Persecution of Iraq's Minorities,' Minority Rights Group International, June 2010.

"Last US troops leave Iraq, ending war." USA Today. 17 December 2011. Retrieved 18 December 2011.

Leigh, David "Carlyle Pulls Out of Iraq Debt Recovery Consortium," Guardian (London), October 15, 2004;

Leigh, Karen. "ISIS Makes up to $3 Million a Day Selling Oil." ABC News. ABC News Network, 2 Aug. 2014. Web. 8 Oct. 2014.

Lemon v. Kurtzman. 403. U.S. 602, 91 S. Ct. 2105, 29 L. Ed. 2d 745 1971 U.S.

"Let's All Go to the Yard Sale," The Economist, September 27, 2003.

Losing Iraq. PBS, 2014. Film.

Luckenbill, D. D. Ancient Records of Assyria and Babylonia, Vol II, (Chicago, 1927).

Makiya, K (1998) [1989], Republic of fear: The politics of modern Iraq. University of California Press.

Malek-Yonan, Rosie. "Quotes-Rosie Malek-Yonan." Rosie Malek-Yonan's Official Website (www.RosieMalek-Yonan.com). Web. 12 Mar. 2015.

Mar Aprem Mooken, The Assyrian Church of the East in the Twentieth Century. Kottayam: St. Ephrem Ecumenical Research Institute, 2003.

Maslow, Abraham H. A Theory of Human Motivation. Psychological Review, 1943. Print.

McCoy, Terrance. "ISIS Just Stole $425 Million, Iraqi Governor Says, and Became the 'world's Richest Terrorist Group'" The Washington Post 12 June 2014. Web. 3 June 2014.

McNeil, William H.; Jean W. Sedlar (1962). The Ancient Near East. OUP.

Mearsheimer, John. The Israel Lobby and U.S. Foreign Policy. Farrar, Straus, and Giroux. 2008. Print.

Middleman, W. "Maslow's Study of Self-actualization." A Reinterpretation of Humanistic Psychology 31 (1991). Print.

Milbank, Dana and Pincus, Walter "U.S. Administrator Imposes Flat Tax System on Iraq," Washington Post, November 2, 2003;

Mill, John Stuart. Utilitarianism, Liberty, Representative Government. London: Everyman's Library, 1910. 243. Print.

Mohammed Mujahid, 'Kidnapped Assyrian Killed in Iraq Despite Ransom Paid.' AINA, 28 August 2010.

Mohammed, Mujahid (AFP), 'Three Christians Killed in North Iraq.' AINA, 17 February 2010. Mujahid 'Five Dead, Including Three Assyrians, in Iraq Attacks,' 24 February 2010.

Moore, Jack. "Mosul Seized: Jihadis Loot $429m from City's Central Bank to Make Isis World's Richest Terror Force.'." International Business Times - International Business News, Financial News, Market News, Politics, Forex, Commodities. 17 June 2014. Web. 19 June 2014.

O'Connel, Mary Ellen. The Power and Purpose of International Law."
Oxford International Press. 2008. "Obama's Speech on Iraq." Council of
Foreign Relations 9 Mar. 2008. Print.

Pedersén, Olof. Archives and Libraries in the Ancient Near East: 1500-300
B.C. Bethesda: CDL Press. 1998

Piketty, Thomas, and Arthur Goldhammer. Capital in the Twenty-first
Century. London: Belknap of Harvard UP, 2014. Print.

Pizzi, Michael. "Obama's Iraq Dilemma." News. 13 June 2014. Web. 3 Mar.
2015.

Poole, Jeffery. "Zarqawi's Pledge of Allegiance to Al-Qaeda." Jamestown
Foundation 18 Oct. 2004. Web. 11 Sept. 2014.

President George W. Bush (January 10, 2007). "President's Address to the
Nation." Office of the Press Secretary.

Pritchard, James B. (1968). The Ancient Near East. OUP.

"RAF Jets Sent on Iraqi Combat Mission." BBC News. 27 Sept. 2014. Web.
21 Oct. 2014.

Raphael Lemkin. EuropeWorld. . Makiya, K (1998) [1989], Republic of fear:
The politics of modern Iraq, University of California Press. June 2001.

"Rare Glimpse Into The Lives of The Assyrian Christians and Yezidis After
The Tragic Attacks of ISIS in Iraq." The Last Plight. Web. 8 Mar. 2015.

Reich, Roebrt B. Saving Capitalism for the Many not the Few. Alfred A.
Knopf. New York. 2015.

Reich, Robert B. The Work of Nations: Preparing Ourselves for 21st-century
Capitalism. New York: First Vintage Edition, 1992.

"The Rump Islamic Emirate of Iraq." The Long War Journal (2006). Web. 2
June 2014.

Rubin, Alissa, and Damian Cave. "In a Force for Iraqi Calm, Seeds of
Conflict." The New York Times 1 Apr. 2004. Web. 5 Sept. 2014.
Saggs, H. The Might that was Assyria (London, 1984).

Saggs, Henry. Everyday Life in Babylonia and Assyria. Assyrian National News Agency. 1965

Said, Edward. Orientalism. Vintage Books. New York. 1989. Pp. 300-301

Schaller, Dominik J. and Zimmerer, Jürgen (2008) "Late Ottoman Genocides: The Dissolution of the Ottoman Empire and Young Turkish population and extermination policies." Journal of Genocide Research, 10:1, pp. 7–14

Shafer, A.T. (1998). The Carving of an Empire: Neo-Assyrian Monuments on the Periphery, p.32-33

Solomon, Erika. "Syria's Jihadist Groups Fight for Control of Eastern Oilfields." The Financial Times 28 Apr. 2014. Web. 17 June 2014.

Spark-Smith, Laura. "More than 100,000 Iraqis Have Fled Their Homes." CNN. Cable News Network, 21 June 2014. Web. 1 Mar. 2015.

Spence, Michael. "The Impact of Globalization on Income and Employment." Foreign Affairs (2011). Vol. 90 Print.

Stafford, R.S. "The Tragedy of the Assyrians" Assyrian International News Agency. 1935

Stiglitz, Joseph. Creating a Learning Society. Columbia University Press. New York. 2014

Stiglitz, Joseph. The Great Divide: Unequal Societies and What we can do about them. New York, NY: Columbia University Press. 2015

Stiglitz, Joseph. Rewriting the rules of the American economy: An Agenda for Growth and shared Prosperity. New York, NY: Columbia University Press. 2015

Tadmor, Hayim, The inscriptions of Tiglath-pileser III, King of Assyria: critical edition, with introductions, translations, and commentary (Jerusalem, Israel Academy of Sciences and Humanities, 1994).

Taylor, Adam. "The Rules in ISIS New State: Amputations for Stealing and Woman to Stay Indoors." The Washington Post 12 June 2014. Print.
"Text of Bush's Speech." CBS News 1 May 2003. Web. 1 May 2006.

The Council of Economic Advisors. "15 Economic facts about Millennials." (2014, October 1). Retrieved August 1, 2015.

"The Executive Life." Fortune 1 Jan. 1956: 30. Print.

"The Jewish Agency for Israel." The Jewish Agency for Israel. Web. 12 Mar. 2015.

The New Fontana Dictionary of Modern Thought, Third Edition. (1999) p. 617.

Travis, Hannibal. Genocide in the Middle East: The Ottoman Empire, Iraq, and Sudan. Durham, North Carolina: Carolina Academic Press, 2010, 2007, pp. 237–77, 293–294.

United Nations Compensation Commission, "Payment of Compensation," press releases, 2005-2006, www.unog.org

"US Official Doubts ISIS Mosul Bank Heist Windfall." NBC News. 24 June 2014. Web. 22 July 2014.

Warda, Joel. "The Flickering Light of Asia" Assyrian International News Agency. 1924.

Warner, Daniel. An Ethic of Responsibility in International Relations. Boulder, Colo.: L. Rienner, 1991. 9-10. Print.

White, Ben. "The Problem with Palestinian Political Leadership." The Guardian, September 1, 2011.

Youash, Michael. "The Tipping Point." Iraqi Sustainable Democracy Project. October 2010

Zucchino, David. "Army Stage-Managed Fall of Hussein Statue." Los Angeles Times 5 July 2004. Web. 5 Mar. 200

www.ingramcontent.com/pod-product-compliance
Lightning Source LLC
Chambersburg PA
CBHW032111280326
41933CB00009B/799